C000125878

Discover
Your True
Potential

R. IAN SEYMOUR

PELICAN PUBLISHING COMPANY
Gretna 2002

One of man's greatest desires is to find meaningful purpose in life and to know that his work is worthwhile.

R. Ian Seymour

Copyright © 2001
By Robert Ian Seymour
All rights reserved

First published by Wrightbooks Pty Ltd, 2001
Published by arrangement with the author by
  Pelican Publishing Company, Inc., 2002

First edition, 2001
First Pelican edition, 2002

The word "Pelican" and the depiction of a pelican are trademarks of Pelican Publishing Company, Inc., and are registered in the U.S. Patent and Trademark Office.

Jacket design by Rob Cowpe

All scripture quotations, unless otherwise indicated, are taken from the *Holy Bible, New International Version. NIV.* Copyright 1973, 1978, 1984 by International Bible Society. Used by permission of Zondervan Publishing House. All rights reserved.

Printed in Canada
Published by Pelican Publishing Company, Inc.
1000 Burmaster Street, Gretna, Louisiana 70053

Contents

*To Kimberley, Aaron and Bethany Faith,
With love from Dad.*

This book was written to help you – as the title says – *Discover Your True Potential.* It is quite simply an inspirational, self-help book written in everyday language to help you, the reader, find true success and happiness in life.

Following the tradition set in the author's previous book, *Maximise Your Potential,* this volume can be considered a follow-up or a sequel, but it has been written in such a way that it can and should be read entirely independently.

Discover Your True Potential is a journey into life. It is a book of encouragement and a blueprint for success, written from experience and with conviction.

Preface

Some of you may remember Robert Ian Collier, a man I once wrote about and who died some 30 years ago. He was a well-liked and highly respected individual who lived a long, happy and very successful life. Robert was a wealthy businessman, but his real passion in life was in the field of self-help and personal development. Robert was also a dedicated family man who just happened to take a shine to me. You see, Robert was my uncle. In fact, I am named after him, although I'm known mostly by my middle name, Ian, rather than Robert.

I lost my own father when I was very young and Uncle Bob, as I used to call him, became my mentor. He was always there to encourage and inspire me and he taught me everything I know about sales, about business and about how to succeed in the game of life. He was my teacher, my personal mentor and my very own Jiminy Cricket. I think that everyone should have an Uncle Bob in his or her life, no matter how old they are, and that's the reason I wrote this book, so that I might pass on what was given to me.

The title of this book is *Discover YOUR True Potential*, with the emphasis on the word 'your'. The reason for this is that I want this book to speak to YOU as an individual and in a personal way. My intention, throughout these pages, is to offer guidance, advice and most of all, encouragement, which is exactly what Uncle Bob, did for me. To help achieve this aim, each chapter is written in the form of a letter from me to you.

Of course, chances are I do not know you personally, although the very fact that you have picked this book up and are now reading these words, tells me that you are a person seeking self-improvement and success; and that being the case, we are at least of kindred spirit. Nonetheless, I still want this book to address you specifically and so I am going to ask you to personalise it for me. Would you turn to the first page of each chapter (page numbers are listed in the Contents) and at the beginning of each letter, where it says, "Dear _ _ _ _ _ _ _ ," take a pen and write in your name, so that my letters are addressed to *you*?

For the duration of your reading, then, I shall take on the role of personal mentor; your Jiminy Cricket or, if you will, your very own Uncle Bob.

(Robert) Ian Seymour
April 2001

Chapter One
The Power of Endurance

*The main difference between a success and a
failure is this: a success is a failure who just kept
on trying!*

Dear _ _ _ _ _ _ _ (fill in your name),

Welcome to this second collection of letters where my intention, once again, is to share with you some further insights for winning and achieving lasting results in this game of life. In this then, the first such letter, I want to talk to you again about persistence, determination and the power of endurance.

You may recall this famous quote from the American poet, Henry Wadsworth Longfellow (1807–1882):

> "Perseverance is a great element of success. If you only knock long enough and loud enough at the gate, you are sure to wake up somebody."

What Longfellow was, in fact, saying is that persistence always conquers resistance, eventually. In this letter I shall demonstrate the power of endurance and show you how, through sustained effort, it is possible for you to attain and, better still, retain lasting success. Welcome then, once again, to what has been referred to as Uncle Bob's 'letters of encouragement'.

Persistence and endurance are key attributes, or characteristics, common to all successful people, no matter what their walk in life. To persist in any endeavour is to have fortitude or staying power and to endure, no matter what the difficulty or how ever long it takes. Of course, when such persistence is properly directed towards a worthwhile endeavour or cause, then a successful outcome is practically always guaranteed. It's important to understand, however, that persistent effort alone does not always equal achievement. Indeed, it is only persistent effort in a feasible or attainable undertaking that guarantees results. For example, I'm sure that you have witnessed the persistent and yet futile attempts of a fly trying to escape through a closed window, when there is an open window just a few feet away. The fly simply doesn't have the capacity to rationalise or determine whether or not the action it is taking is appropriate. So the fly continues in its fight for survival and keeps on flying into the window pane until it eventually dies of exhaustion – either that or brain damage! So you can see, then, that persistent effort alone does not always achieve the desired results.

I'm sure that you can relate to a similar situation where you've dug your heels in and persisted in an endeavour, only to find out that you've been hitting your head against a brick wall and getting nowhere fast! In such circumstances we need to take stock and ask ourselves whether or not what we are attempting to achieve is a feasible undertaking. Is it attainable or not? And if it is attainable, is this present course of action the right one to take or do you need to change direction? Remember, persistent effort alone does not always equal results. You also need to plan properly and have the necessary tools available to work with.

To illustrate this point further, consider the story of the lumberjack who increased his efforts to fell more trees. The lumberjack worked harder than he had ever done before but at the end of the day, it was his productivity that fell and not more trees. You see, although the lumberjack increased his efforts, although he threw himself into his task and persisted in his toil all day long, he didn't take the time to sharpen his axe! He didn't take stock or plan properly. From this tale you can see that sheer determination alone can, and often will, achieve results but, of course, those results will always be far more effective when your efforts have proper direction.

Persistence alone, then, is no guarantee of success. It is only when we persist with direction and a purpose in mind that we achieve results. I once read of an experiment conducted by the famous French naturalist and Nobel Prize winner, Jean Henri Fabre (1823–1915). The experiment studied the behaviour of a certain type of caterpillar, termed the 'processionary caterpillar' – so named because when one of the caterpillars moves off in a certain direction, the others follow suit and fall in closely behind the caterpillar in front. In the experiment Fabre enticed one of the caterpillars to crawl around the rim of a large flowerpot. He then introduced other caterpillars to follow the leader until there were so many caterpillars along the rim of the flowerpot that it was no longer possible to distinguish which caterpillar was at the head and which was at the tail of the procession. The caterpillars, oblivious to their futile effort, continued to crawl around the rim following the caterpillar in front for several days until eventually, one by one, they fell off the flowerpot through exhaustion and lack of food. From this experiment we can see, once again, that activity or persistent effort does not necessarily equate to achievement. Sometimes we need to know when to persist and sometimes we need to know when to let go and change direction.

So how can people determine when to persist in their endeavours and when to actually give up and change direction? In attempting to answer that question there are several points I'd like to make. Firstly, you are the only person who can ultimately decide whether or not you are embarked on the right path and whether or not your present course of action is achievable. If you're not sure, my advice is to seek the opinion of a mentor or someone who will give you an honest and unbiased opinion. Secondly, you need to ask yourself questions such as:

- Is this something I enjoy doing?
- Am I competent in what I am doing?
- Am I improving and moving forward?
- Is there a worthwhile purpose to it?
- Do I honestly believe, that in following this course of action, I will succeed?
- Overall, is this something that will be constructive or destructive to my future plans?

Once you have answered these questions you then need to take action. In other words, you need to stop deliberating about it and either do it, delegate it or dump it! In a nutshell, then, if you are into something get into it and if you are not into it, get out! This leads me on to my next point, which is this: never give in to discouragement. Never. Never. Never! Understand that discouragement is the biggest killer of achievement known to man. If you contemplate giving up because you feel discouraged my advice to you is very simply this: DON'T QUIT! I know that is easy to say but understand this: it's often when we feel discouraged and want to quit that success is looming just around the next corner. As an analogy, consider for a moment that the sky is always the darkest just before dawn. (This happens because – as the moon is about to set and the sun about to rise – there is no reflected light in the heavens.) In other words, it has to get dark before it gets light. So don't ever stop because you are discouraged or because things look bleak, instead grit your teeth, push on and persevere anticipating the dawn. Just keep on keeping on and remember this: you may be in a storm, but no matter how thick or dark the clouds are, climb up through them and the sun is still shining brightly.

Let's assume, for the moment, that you know what you want and you're on the right track; I want to turn now and look at the value and power behind sustained and persistent effort. Consider Niagara Falls on the borders of New York State in the United States, and the province of Ontario in Canada. Niagara Falls is one of the largest and most impressive waterfalls in the world. The sheer volume of water passing over the falls and the power generated from it is enormous. For example, every minute some 340,000 cubic metres of water pours over the falls. That's enough to fill about 700 Olympic-sized swimming pools or the equivalent to 385,000 tonnes of water every minute of every hour of every day. Such a vast amount of water generates enough power to accommodate, altogether, six hydroelectric plants, which produce some 3½ million kilowatts of electricity.

Now, without question, that's a great deal of power, but here's my point: for all its beauty and impressiveness, Niagara Falls, in fact every waterfall, started out in life as a single drop of water! Think about it. A single drop of water mingles with another and another to form a small puddle or pool. The pool then converges with other pools and begins to trickle downhill as a tiny stream. Other streams then come together and form a river. Finally, as the river continues downhill towards the sea it combines with others and the end result is a massive expanse of water such as the Niagara

4

River and Falls. And all this from a single drop of water and the relentless persistence of other similar drops. Likewise, then, with you. No matter where you start from or however little you start with, providing you are heading in the right direction with relentless persistence, you too, over time, can and will achieve amazing and impressive results – if you do not give up.

The film star turned producer, Sylvester Stallone, famed for the *Rocky* films, knows the power of endurance. He once said, "I'm not the smartest or most talented person in the world, but I succeeded because I kept going and going and going." This statement is true of all successful people. You see, like Sylvester Stallone, it takes years of sustained effort to become an overnight success! These are sentiments that are echoed in the now frequently quoted words of Thomas Edison, taken from a 1932 edition of *Life* magazine:

> "Genius is one per cent inspiration and ninety-nine per cent perspiration."

Again, what Edison was promoting was the power of endurance.

Sir Winston Churchill (1874–1965) was nicknamed 'the British Bulldog' because of his stubborn tenacity, his will to win and his sheer persistence, especially in the face of overwhelming odds during the bleakest hours of World War II. And thank goodness that he was persistent, otherwise the world in which we now live might very well have been a completely different place. Referring to his media image as the British bulldog and at the same time defining perseverance, Churchill once said:

> "The nose of the bulldog has been slanted backwards so that he can breathe without letting go."

Now, that's what I call a picture of tenacity and persistence.

Unfortunately though, persistence is not an attribute that simply comes naturally to us. That is to say, persistence is not an easily acquired trait. It requires discipline and character to persevere in our endeavours. The plain fact is, just as water or electricity follows the path of least resistance so too we, as human beings, have a tendency to do the same thing. Certainly, we all desire to be successful but for the most part, the majority of people are not prepared to put in the effort required to achieve the results. Most folk have good intentions and most start out well enough, but at the first sign of difficulty they quit. A humorist once put it this way:

> "Failure has been correctly identified as the path of least persistence."

That's very true. Success, on the other hand, can be correctly identified as the path of *most* persistence.

For those of you who have read my previous book, *Maximise Your Potential*, you will be aware of my affection for the English-born (American-bred) poet, Edgar A. Guest (1881–1959), who wrote many simple, yet very profound and inspirational, verses. Here's one that I'd like to share with you and which relates very well to this subject of endurance.

No One is Beat 'til He Quits

No one is beat 'til he quits,
No one is through 'til he stops,
No matter how failure hits,
No matter how often he drops.
See, a fellar's not down 'til he lies
In the dust and refuses to rise.

Fate can slam him and bang him around,
And batter his frame 'til he's sore,
But it never can say that he's downed,
While he bobs up serenely for more.
See a fellar's not dead 'til he dies,
Nor beat 'til he no longer tries.

Edgar A. Guest

In the Bible it says, "A man reaps what he sows" (Galatians 6:7). A few lines further on it says, "Let us not become weary in doing good, for at the proper time we will reap a harvest if we do not give up." (Galatians 6:9) The apostle, Paul, wrote those words almost 2000 years ago. What Paul was saying is that, if whatever you are doing is good or beneficial to yourself or others, if it's worthwhile, then stick with it, persist and eventually you'll come through and receive your just rewards.

The famous English theologian, Charles Spurgeon (1834–1892), when talking about endurance, said, "It was by perseverance that the snail reached the ark." And that is of course true in any worthwhile endeavour. It's continuity that counts. You have to put in the persistent effort if you want to reap the rewards. It's the constant drip, drip, drip of the water that has the power to bore through solid rock!

Staying on the theme of boring through solid rock, did you know that on average it takes 254 tonnes of rock to produce a single diamond? Each diamond, once it's been refined, is then sorted into 1 of 5,000 categories based on the carat, colour, clarity and cut of the precious stone. Now, that's an awful lot of work for one diamond but then, look at how valuable diamonds are! To everything there is a cost. The question is, are you willing to pay the price? Are you willing to put in the time and effort and whatever else is necessary to succeed? There's a wise old adage that says: "To get whatever you want, do whatever it takes."

So far, we have been looking at the positive effects of persistent effort and determination but I now want to turn for a moment or two and warn you briefly about the negative effects or the danger of misdirected persistence. Understand that any and all persistent effort produces a degree of results but those results don't necessarily have to be positive. Take, for example, someone who is a constant worrier. Now, of course, everyone worries from time to time but the sort of person I'm talking about here worries about every little thing. Even when there is absolutely nothing to actually worry about, the constant worrier is the kind of person who becomes worried that things are running too smoothly! Here, the power of endurance obviously has a negative effect and the results are unhappiness, ulcers, high blood pressure and worse. You know, worrying is actually futile. It's like being on a rocking chair: try as hard as you like it won't get you anywhere!

Let me give you another illustration of the negative effects of persistence, as told by the late Dr Harry Emerson Fosdick (1878–1969), the US clergyman and educator:

"On the slope of Long's Peak [in the Rocky Mountains] in Colorado lies the ruin of a gigantic tree. Naturalists tell us that it stood for some 400 years. It was a seedling when Columbus landed at San Salvador [Bahamas], and half grown when the Pilgrims settled at Plymouth [Massachusetts]. During the course of its long life it was struck by lightning 14 times, and the innumerable avalanches and storms of four centuries thundered past it. It survived them all. In the end, however, an army of beetles attacked the tree and levelled it to the ground. The insects ate their way through the bark and gradually destroyed the inner strength of the tree by their tiny but incessant attacks. A forest giant which age had not withered, nor lightning blasted, nor storms subdued, fell at last before beetles so small that a man could crush them between his forefinger and his thumb." [1]

It's important to understand both the positive and negative power of persistence. You must determine never to allow discouragement or negativity to eat away at you, like the beetles eating away at that giant tree. Remember, persistence always conquers resistance eventually, so make sure that you use persistence to work for you and not against you.

Moving on, it's important to also understand that the winners in life are not necessarily the most gifted or talented of people. Nor is success anything to do with luck or good fortune. Neither is it necessarily anything to do with having more than a fair share of intelligence or brains. No! It's not so much good fortune or intelligence that counts: what really matters is individual talent coupled with a positive attitude. Winners persist and succeed in life because they have the right attitude – which is the topic of my next letter. For now though, here's another verse based around the theme of trying and persistent effort. Read it often and be encouraged to persevere.

The Man Who Wins

The man who wins is an average man,
Not built on any particular plan;
Not blessed with any particular luck,
Just steady and earnest and full of pluck.
The man who wins is the man who works,
Who neither labour nor trouble shirks;
Who uses his hands, his head, his eyes.
The man who wins is the man who tries.

Anonymous

Well, by now I think you've got the message loud and clear. The winners in life are those individuals who have developed the

1. *How to Stop Worrying and Start Living* by Dale Carnegie, (1953) Cedar Books, London, p. 81–82.

attributes or characteristics of endurance and persistence. Just as we can't tell which is the straw that breaks the camel's back, likewise we can't tell which of our efforts is the one that will succeed. It might just very well be on the next try. In conclusion then, I want to encourage you again, to keep on keeping on. Remember also to be on your guard against discouragement and pay little attention to its voice. Bear in mind that a quitter never wins and a winner never quits. So don't be a one-day hero: a hero for today and then a zero for tomorrow. Don't be a one-day wonder – be consistent by being persistent. Stick with it, Go-getter.

Yours cordially,
Uncle Bob

Chapter Two
Attitude and Positive Thinking

The most important conversations you have all day long are the ones you have with yourself.

Dear _ _ _ _ _ _ _ (fill in your name),

Nowadays it's generally accepted, although not as widely practised, that you have to believe and have faith in your ability to win, before you ever can win. You have to anticipate and expect success before you can ever achieve any measure of it. The plain fact is if you want to win in this game of life then you have to think positive, act positive and be positive. In other words you have to be an optimist.

When it comes to achieving real and lasting success the 'secret formula' is found in this saying: "Your attitude in life almost always determines your altitude in life." In this letter we shall be looking first of all at attitude, before moving on to discuss the 'know-how' or the 'how-to' of positive thinking and the associated benefits.

Let me begin with a story about contrasting attitudes. There was once a pair of twins who were identical in appearance but were complete opposites in everything else. One of the boys was a prophet of doom and gloom, a despairing pessimist in almost everything he did. In complete contrast the other boy was an unmistakable optimist whose enthusiasm for life was unquenchable. The huge disparity between the twins became a cause of concern to their parents and so they decided to seek the advice of an eminent psychiatrist. The psychiatrist suggested that treating the boys differently could rectify the imbalance. With Christmas coming up he suggested the parents gave the children different gifts. "Give the pessimist the best toys you can afford but give the optimist nothing but a box of manure," he said, "This will help to balance out their attitudes."

When Christmas morning came around the parents observed the children opening their presents. The pessimist opened his first. He ripped off the wrapping paper from a very large box and discovered inside a brand new bicycle. "Oh, I don't like it!" he immediately moaned. "It's the wrong colour, it's too big and I'd probably fall off and injure myself." He discarded the bicycle and opened another present. This time he revealed the latest personal computer with several games and software packages. "I don't like this either," he complained, "Computers are too complicated. It takes too long to work the keyboard and I've never been any good with a joystick! Besides, it'll probably just keep breaking down, either that or the glare from the computer screen will hurt my eyes!" The parents, dismayed, turned to watch the optimist as he opened his one and only present. Excitedly, he tore off the paper and opened the box. Then, jumping for joy and throwing handfuls of manure in the air, he shouted gleefully, "Yippee ... hooray ... whoopee ...! You can't fool me, where is it? Where is it?" The parents looked at him with a puzzled expression only to hear him declare, "With this much manure there's got to be a pony around here somewhere!"

Now, you might smile but the moral behind this little tale is clear: our attitude, or the way we think, affects our behaviour. Our behaviours, if repeated, become habits and our habits become a way of life. Both optimism and pessimism are learned behaviours; that is to say, our behaviour is not inherent, compulsive or down to chance or fate but, rather, it is a chosen response. We choose or determine what our attitudes and responses will be. For example, a man applies but fails to get a promotion at work. How does he respond? Well, he has a choice. He can let the bad news and disappointment get to him, in which case it will have an adverse effect on his job and maybe even his health or career or worse! Alternatively, he can choose to put it down to experience and then bounce straight back into action again, determined to win the next time around. It is just a question of choice! So you see, it's not so much what happens to you but rather, it's how you react to what happens to you that makes all the difference. A philosopher once defined the difference between an optimist and a pessimist like this: "An optimist laughs to forget but a pessimist forgets to laugh."

Understand this: whether you expect the best and are optimistic or you expect the worst and are pessimistic, you are sending out an invitation and you can be sure you will receive a reply. Why? Because expectations are never fussy about whose table they sit at, and they've never been known to decline an invitation! Let me put it this way: *your expectations eventually become your manifestations.* So then, look after your inner self – force yourself to be optimistic if you have to – and you ultimately look after your outer self! Now, of course, it's not always easy being optimistic. In fact, sometimes it's very difficult to remain upbeat and positive. But if you hang in there, if you continue to try and don't give up, then in the end you will invariably find that the rewards are worth the effort. Remember, persistence always conquers resistance, eventually. In summary then, the only real difference between lasting success or failure (not fleeting success or failure) is a difference in attitude.

So how can a person change his or her attitude from negative to positive? How can a person become an optimist? And how can we remain positive when things go wrong? Well, the best way I know of acquiring a lasting and overall positive attitude in life, is to develop an attitude of gratitude, or as my late grandmother would have said, "always count your blessings".

Zig Ziglar, the best-selling author and inspirational speaker, puts it like this:

> "The more you thank God for what you have, the more you will have to thank God for."

Now, of course, being grateful for your blessings and having a positive attitude will not necessarily bring about every desire of your heart (just as the boy in the story didn't get the pony), but life is always far kinder to the thankful optimist. And consider this: how many pessimists or negative people do you know who are happy, healthy and successful in life? Not a single one, I'm sure! The reason for this is down to what's known as 'the universal law of attraction,' which basically says, what you think about comes about, be it positive or negative.

Benjamin Franklin, on the subject of attitude, wrote:

> "Blessed is he who expects nothing, for he shall never be disappointed."

And on a contrasting note the famous writer, W. Somerset Maugham (1874–1965), once said:

> "It's a funny thing life. If you refuse to accept anything but the best, you often get it."

Let me ask you, what do you expect from life? I believe with all my heart that God intended man to flourish, to find purpose and fulfilment, which is something far deeper than mere material wealth. In fact, of all the animals that have ever lived on the earth, as far as we know man is the only one, the only solitary animal, who is not governed by instinct. Instead, man is governed by his own free will. We have the freedom of choice. From birth every other animal survives by instinct, which is somehow biologically programmed into its very being. But man is different.

The Bible tells us:

> "God created man in his own image, in the image of God he created him; male and female." (Genesis 1:27)

So, you see, man is creative by design and he is also distinguished from the other animals by having freedom of choice; he has a free will to choose as he pleases. It is, therefore, left up to each individual to determine his or her own attitude, to determine which path to choose in life and how high to climb. Remember, "Your attitude almost always determines your altitude in life." If you seek prosperity, happiness and fulfilment in life (and don't we all) then you need to seek them expecting that you will find them. In essence, what I am saying is this: you will only get out of life what you put into life and what you expect to receive from it. Success, then, doesn't simply fall into your lap by accident; rather it is something that you have to work towards with expectation. The words in the following verse, written by Jessie B. Rittenhouse (1869–1948), reinforce this message.

My Wage

I bargained with life for a penny,
And life would pay no more,
However I begged at evening,
When I counted my scanty score.
For life is a just employer,
Who gives you what you ask,
But once you have set the wages,
Why, then you must bear the task.
I worked for a menial's hire,
Only to learn, dismayed,
That any wage I had asked of life,
Life would have willingly paid.

Jessie B. Rittenhouse

Indeed, life always has an uncanny way of giving us whatever we ask for, albeit we might ask subliminally. What you see is what you get. What you see yourself as, is what you become. See yourself as only worth mediocre pay and that's all you'll ever earn. But see yourself worthy of a great deal more and ... well, the sky's your limit. Success depends upon a positive attitude. Think of it like this: if you approach any endeavour without a PMA (Positive Mental Attitude) you'll always be DOA (Dead On Arrival or else Defeated On Attempting!).

There's an old story told about a professor who was studying people's different attitudes to work. One day the professor went to a construction site and spoke with three labourers who were laying bricks. "What are you doing?" he asked the first man. "Hey, I'm just a bricklayer. I'm only doing what I've been told to do," came the reply. "If you've got a problem with that go and see the foreman over there!" The professor smiled politely and moved on to ask the same question of a second man. "Well I know it's a bit mundane and it's not much of a job, but it pays $18 an hour and I've got bills to pay just like everyone else so I'm not complaining." The professor thanked the man and moved on to ask someone else. In the distance he noticed a man intent on his work so he walked over and said, "Excuse me. What are you doing?" The bricklayer looked up, smiled and with a gleam in his eye said, "Why, can't you see? I'm building a cathedral." Three men all doing the same job but with three different attitudes. Let me say it again: *your attitude in life almost always determines your altitude in life.*

In a moment we're going to look at the practice of positive thinking but before we do here's a final story which gives a beautiful illustration of someone with a positive attitude. There was once a poverty-stricken old lady who was so poor that she didn't have any money to buy food. The one thing she did have, however, was a positive attitude and complete faith that God would provide for her. So she did the only thing she could do. She got down on her knees and prayed over and over in a loud voice, "Father in Heaven, please send me some bread and vegetables so that I can eat." Now it just so happened that as she was praying the local scoundrel was passing by her window, and overhearing the old woman's plea for help, decided to play a trick on her. He dashed off to the nearest store and purchased some bread and vegetables. Then, returning to the old woman's house, he climbed a ladder and dropped the food down the chimney, whereupon it landed right in front of the woman as she was praying. "Oh thank you Lord, thank you!" she cried out again and again as she gathered up the groceries. Then, overcome with excitement, she ran out into the street and began enthusiastically telling everyone what had happened and how God had answered her prayers. This was just too much for the scoundrel and, unable to contain himself, he fell about laughing wildly and began poking fun at the old woman. Mocking her publicly he told the people crowding around that it was he and not God who had dropped the food down the chimney. The old woman looked at him, continued to smile and without missing a beat replied, "Well the devil may have brought it but it was God who sent it!" Now that's what I call a positively heavenly attitude!

Moving on, I want to look now at the principles of positive thinking and show you, as best I can, how our thoughts have a magnetic influence that attracts that which we think about, be it positive or negative.

Let me tell you another story. During a party recently, someone asked me that age-old question, "What do you do for a living?" Always the opportunist looking for new business I replied, "I work in the futures market." A stockbroker friend, overhearing me, gave me a surprised glance, but then smiled as I continued, "I work in the futures market in that I encourage, teach and motivate people to enjoy a happier and more successful tomorrow!"

Mostly, I'm a very positive person (we all have our off days), but sometimes I'll meet a sceptic who doesn't advocate my own views on positive thinking or attitude. I've often been asked questions such as: "You don't really believe that you can change a situation just by thinking positively about it, do you?" My answer is always, "No, I don't!" You see, it's not just positive thinking: it also takes positive action. The important thing to remember here is that thought always precedes action. Always!

It's been said, "A man is not what he thinks he is, but what he thinks – he is!" That's so very true. If you think positive, have a great attitude and expect to succeed, you will eventually succeed. But similarly, if you have a lousy attitude or you suffer from what's been termed, 'Stickin' thinkin',' (negative thinking) you won't.

Here's an example. Suppose you wanted to be a fruit farmer. If you did, you wouldn't go off to Antarctica to plant your orchards, would you? Why not? Well, Antarctica simply isn't the right environment to produce fruit in, is it? Likewise then, if you want to be successful and produce 'fruit' in your own life, you must first of all sow the seeds (positive thoughts) in a fertile environment (your own mind).

Now, I'm the first to admit that thinking positive and having a great attitude does not and cannot create miracles. For example, no matter how hard I tried, I couldn't move a solid object, such as a rock, just with the power of thought. The fact is, if I want to move a rock I also need to take some action. Let me say it again, thought always precedes action. And when your thoughts are positive you stand a far better chance of success than you otherwise would.

A positive attitude is the chrysalis of success. Listen to the words of Vince Lombardi (1913–1970), the famous American football coach who became a national symbol of determination and accomplishment:

> "Winning isn't everything, but wanting to win is."

> "The difference between a successful person and others is not a lack of strength, not a lack of knowledge, but rather a lack of will."

Now that's a PMA, a positive mental attitude. Someone else who was a lifetime student of positive thinking was Napoleon Hill, author of the 20-million-plus best-selling book *Think and Grow Rich*. Here's a well-known quote from the book:

"Whatever the mind of man can conceive and believe it will achieve."

There are many different ways of stating that sentiment. Personally, I like to put it like this: what you think about comes about!

But how does it work? How does our thinking attract or bring about the very thing that we are thinking about? What happens? There is a human tendency to try and break everything down so that we are able to explain things and understand exactly how they work. We want to put everything in a box and be able to label them or, at the very least, be able to systemise things into some sort of rational order. The problem with the 'magnetic force' surrounding our thoughts and attitudes is that it's very difficult to understand how it works. For years scientists have been trying to unravel and explain the capacity and power of the human mind but they have never been able to do so. This is partly, I suppose, because this force is not tangible, you can't see it, although you can see its effects or consequences. Claude M. Bristol, author of another classic book, *The Magic of Believing*, puts it like this:

"While man hasn't been able to define it, manifestations of thought attraction can be seen on every hand. It is like the electrical field itself – we do not know what electricity is, although in a material sense we know how we can generate it through various kinds of energy-producing apparatus."

Likewise then, when it comes down to our thoughts and attitudes attracting that which we are constantly thinking about, we don't have to know exactly how it works or indeed, what makes it work, to know that it does, in fact, work.

You'll notice in the above paragraph that I wrote we attract that which we *constantly* think about. It's not as if our every passing thought materialises into the corresponding result. You have to focus and remain focused on your objective. It's like going out into the garden on a hot and sunny day with a magnifying glass and a piece of paper with the intention of starting a fire. If you keep shifting the magnifying glass around from one place to another, nothing happens. But if you hold the magnifying glass still and focus on one position, you then harness the sun's powerful rays and before you know it you've started a fire. The same applies with our thinking. When we remain focused (positively or negatively) the object of our thinking eventually materialises.

Let me put it like this: our minds are storehouses of such potential power that it literally is mind-boggling what man can achieve when he puts his mind to it! (Excuse the pun.) It's this same 'mind power' which is responsible for every single thing that you can see around you at this moment, everything that is man-made, that is. Think about it. Everything that is man-made originally started out in life as a thought in the mind of someone. Indeed, it is the power of the human mind which is responsible for the technology that today allows man to soar to great heights and walk on another planet, or plunge to great depths and explore the ocean floor, or perform intricate microsurgery on another human being. Some individuals have trained and developed their minds to such an extent that they can now achieve incredible feats. Take, for example, the current record-breaking memorist, Dominic O'Brien, who in August 1996 set a new world record in memory accomplishment. Mr O'Brien was given a number of shuffled packs of playing cards and set the task of memorising as many cards as possible in the right sequence and within a set time limit of one hour. The result was truly amazing. Mr O'Brien scored 710 points, or to be more precise, he remembered and correctly identified the sequence of 13.6 packs of pre-shuffled playing cards in a time span of just 60 minutes!

Let me now introduce you to a very clever friend of mine who does a lot of my thinking, remembering and problem-solving for me. He's an imaginary friend, in fact, an ancient Roman philosopher (a great thinker) who goes by the name of Myus Subconscious. Whenever I have a problem or I want to remember something, I speak to my very own thinker, philosopher and good friend, Myus Subconscious. I simply hand the situation over to him and ask him to come up with a solution for me. Now, providing that my mind or memory bank has, at one time or another, received the required information that I'm looking for, then Myus Subconscious will more often than not come up with the answer for me!

Let me move off at a tangent for a moment and try to explain, from a layman's point of view, what happens. Scientists estimate that we have over a trillion nerve cells or *neurons* in our brain. This means that we have the capacity of recording to memory almost every stimulus received from each of our five senses (sight, sound, smell, taste and touch) throughout our entire life. In other words, our mind has the capability of recording and storing every piece of information ever given to it, without any conscious effort on our part.

My understanding, however, is that the brain loses or discards *some* of the irrelevant information which is recorded in our short-term memory. The rest of the information is filed away in the depths of our trillion-plus archive of neurons. It may seem lost forever, but it is still in there somewhere! Indeed, there are many examples of this being the case. One such example is given by Maxwell Maltz, MD, in his best-selling book, *Psycho-Cybernetics*. Dr Maltz records a discovery made by another doctor, Dr Wilder Penfield, then the director of the Montreal Neurological Institute. During a brain operation on a female patient who was wide awake, Dr Penfield happened to touch a small area of the cortex with a surgical instrument, which then stimulated an amazing response. The woman immediately exclaimed that she was reliving an incident from her childhood that she had completely forgotten about. Note that the term used was 'reliving,' as though the actual incident had been recorded on video and was now being played back! I can remember hearing of a similar incident, of a woman (maybe even the same one) who was given a slight electrical stimulus and began reliving her fifth birthday party, right down to seeing her childhood friends, the dresses that they wore, the smell and taste of the birthday cake, etc. (As I recall the source of this latter example is Denis Waitley's audio programme, *The Psychology of Winning*.)

I can't say that I have ever experienced anything so dramatic, nor would I ever want to! But I am very often pleasantly surprised with the results from my very own Myus Subconscious. Let me explain. If I'm trying to remember a name or a face, or I'm looking for the answer to a problem or even some fresh inspiration or ideas for my writing, speaking or training seminars, whatever it might be, if I'm stuck I simply take my question or problem and hand it over to Myus to think about for me. This allows me, or should I say, my conscious self, to get on with other more productive things.

As the French writer Voltaire (1694–1778) once put it, "No problem can withstand the assault of sustained thinking." For myself, it works rather like this. I give Myus Subconscious a command, much the same as I would give a command to a computer, except that I say it aloud for extra impact. Myus often seems to have a mind of his own and sometimes he even seems to be a bit moody! I always try, therefore, to be extra polite to him (he is my room-mate, after all) and very often I have to be patient and wait for him to respond. Over the years I've discovered that one of the best times to ask a favour of him is just before I retire at night. It seems that he, generally, likes to work best when my conscious self sleeps.

Let me give you an illustration. A moment ago I gave an example taken from the book *Psycho-Cybernetics* by Dr Maxwell Maltz. I remembered reading about this woman's operation and her amazing story but I couldn't (consciously) remember where I had read about it. (My personal library contains several hundred books.) I wanted to share the story with you but as I couldn't remember the full details or the source I asked Myus to help me out. The command simply went like this: "Where did I read about this woman's story? What is the source?" Then I put the problem to the back of my mind and went off to have lunch with my wife, Suzanne (leaving my subconscious in search mode). In this particular instance I didn't have to wait very long. As soon as I sat down to eat lunch the answer suddenly came to me. I was given the name of the book, the author and even whereabouts in the book the story would be found (at the beginning on a left-hand page).

Our subconscious mind can work not just to retrieve lost information but, as I've already said, also in matters requiring creative inspiration or decision-making. I can't, however, promise that you'll always get the desired results just by using your mental abilities. Furthermore, I am not foolhardy enough to pretend to know all the answers ... but, as the saying goes, I know someone who does! As far as I, and many millions of others, are concerned, there is someone who knows everything and has all the answers, and that someone is God. Whenever I'm not sure what to do or I can't find the solution to a particular problem by myself, I pray about it. And I don't mind telling you, God has never let me down.

Going back to what I said earlier, we have each been given our own free will. Our lives are not controlled by instinct, but rather, we have the freedom of choice to determine our own way. We have the capacity for independent and creative thought and our thoughts, as we have seen, have that magnetic quality of attracting that which we *constantly* think about.

The English author, James Allen (1864–1912), used part of a proverb (Proverbs 23:7) from the King James Version of the Bible as the title for his phenomenal bestselling book, *As a Man Thinketh*. In the book Allen wrote:

> "As a man thinketh in his heart so he is. This not only embraces the whole of a man's being, but also is so comprehensive as to reach out to every condition and circumstance of his life. A man is literally what he thinks, his character being the complete sum of all his thoughts."

In summary, our thoughts – our constant thoughts, that is – attract the very things that we think about.

Now, we can control our thoughts, that much is fact. And another fact is this: it is only possible to think one thought at a time. Bearing this in mind, then, here's some good advice. Whenever you become consciously aware of having a negative thought, you can control it; you can forcibly change the thought for a positive one. It's this very same principle of only being able to think one thought at a time that makes counting sheep so effective in sending you to sleep at night. When your body is tired but your mind is running on overdrive with all the whys and worries of the day, the problems and concerns for tomorrow or even in excited anticipation of forthcoming events, counting sheep forcibly stops you from thinking about other things. Since you can only think one thought at a time – and let's be honest, sheep are rather boring – you fall asleep.

Let me say it once again, *you can choose your thoughts.* You can choose to think positively; you can choose to make 'it' happen, because your thoughts have the power of attracting whatever it is that you earnestly desire. The easiest and most effective way of utilising this 'thought power' is through positive self-talk, or *affirmations.* The novelist, Jonathan Swift (1667–1745), wrote: "Vision is the art of seeing the invisible." That's what you must do: see the invisible. Repeat positive affirmations to yourself over and over, say them with conviction, and at the same time visualise a successful outcome as having already happened, in the past tense. This is very important because if you visualise something as going to happen, in the future tense, then it always will remain that way – in the future!

Let me finish off this letter by reminding you, once again, that in order to enjoy success in life you have to think positive and act positive. In other words, it's not just positive thinking that achieves the results, it's also taking positive action and usually lots of it! James Allen also wrote:

> "Not what he wishes and prays for does a man get, but what he justly earns. His wishes and prayers are only gratified and answered when they harmonise with his thoughts and actions."

Some of you might recall this short poem that I shared in *Maximise Your Potential* which fittingly illustrates this point about winning requiring our positive acts as well as our positive thoughts:

> When God created us, he gave us two ends,
> One to sit on and one to think with.
> Success depends upon which end we most use,
> Heads we win and tails we lose!

Having now looked at the power of persistence, attitude and positive thinking, it is, indeed, time to take action. In my next letter to you, I shall be looking at purpose: finding it, defining it and achieving it. Until next time then, I remain,

Yours cordially,
Uncle Bob

Chapter Three

Purpose

One of man's greatest desires is to find meaningful purpose in life and to know that his work is worthwhile.

Dear _ _ _ _ _ _ (fill in your name),

There comes a time when each of us begins to question the meaning of life, the reason for our being here or the purpose for our existence. We ask the questions: "Why do I feel so unsatisfied? Will I ever achieve fulfilment? Will my life be meaningful and worthwhile? Will my having lived make a difference? Will I ever find significance, happiness and contentment?" As people look around they see others who seem to have it 'all together,' and many ask: "Why them and not me?"

It seems that people tend to spend the first half of their lives seeking riches and success and the second half seeking direction and purpose. In fact, in the middle of *life* is the word 'if' – and that seems to be the conundrum for most people: "If I could only find my real purpose in life," they say. Of course, some do find it, but there are many who don't. The unfortunate ones, who don't, become lost and weary. They tend to go through life lacking energy and vitality and become more and more cynical and discontented. They also tend to seem much older than their years!

In this letter then, I have two objectives. The first is to, hopefully, point you in the right direction and help you discover your calling and purpose in life, if you don't already know what that is. (If you are already aware of your purpose, then my aim is to both reaffirm that awareness and encourage you onwards.) My second objective is to offer some constructive advice and to help you plan your journey more effectively.

First off then, is purpose. Humanity has always cried out for fulfilment. We have a basic human need to feel significant, to feel wanted, loved and appreciated. It's true that our family, friends and work do give meaning to our lives and, indeed, life itself would be utterly intolerable without them. But even with such things, people still seek their place in the world, their niche, role or calling.

The law of averages tells us that during a typical lifetime a person will sleep for about 23 years; spend around six years watching television; about three years eating and drinking; another three years getting either dressed or undressed and around nine months in the bathroom! Now, there must be more to life than this, and there is. It's called purpose.

As a Christian, I believe that people find true purpose only when they seek God through the life and teachings of Jesus Christ. This book wasn't written, nor is it intended to be, a religious book, as such. But, as I've already said, it is my intention to point you in the right direction, and the way that I and millions of others see it, belief in God offers the only real explanation for our existence. It also offers a destiny and the promise of eternal life, which for the Christian are, indeed, the very reason for life.

However, although belief in God provides a reason for life, it does not necessarily reveal our individual purpose or calling in life. That is something entirely different and something that each one of us must discover for him or herself. There are nevertheless some very definite clues that can point us in the right direction and we shall look at these in a moment or two. First of all though, read what some of the world's most accomplished people, both past and present, have had to say on this subject of purpose.

- **Thomas Carlyle (1795–1881), Scottish historian and philosopher:**
  "A man without a purpose is like a ship without a rudder."

- **William James (1842–1910), US philosopher and psychologist:**
  "The deepest principle in human nature is the craving to be appreciated."

- ◆ *Mack R. Douglas, best-selling author:*
  "The greatest use of life is to so use your life that the use of your life will outlive your life."

- ◆ *Harold Kushner, rabbi and author:*
  "Our souls are not hungry for fame, comfort, wealth or power. Those rewards create almost as many problems as they solve. Our souls are hungry for meaning, so that our lives matter, and our world will at least be a little bit better for our having passed through it."

- ◆ *Confucius (551–479 BC), Chinese philosopher and teacher:*
  "Choose a job you love and you will never have to work a day in your life."

- ◆ *Benjamin Franklin (1706–1790), US statesman, scientist and author:*
  "Don't hide your talents; they for use were made: / What's the use of a sundial if it's kept in the shade?"

- ◆ *Henry Wadsworth Longfellow (1807–1882), US poet:*
  "The talent of success is nothing more than doing what you can do well, and doing well whatever you do."

- ◆ *John Ruskin (1819–1900), British writer, art critic and social reformer:*
  "The highest reward for man's toil is not what he gets for it but what he becomes by it."

- ◆ *Sir James M. Barrie (1860–1937), dramatist and novelist:*
  "The secret of being happy is not in doing what one likes, but in liking what one does."

- ◆ *Leo Calvin Rosten (1908–1997), Polish-born American author:*
  "I think the purpose of life is to be happy, to be useful, to be responsible, to be honourable, to be compassionate. It is above all, to matter, to count, to stand for something, to have made some difference that you have lived at all."

All of the above quotes and words of wisdom suggest that happiness, success and fulfilment come, not from obtaining power or wealth, but from finding your individual purpose and then making that purpose your life's work. So how does a person find his or her purpose? Unfortunately, there is no easy answer to that question, but if I had to sum it up in one sentence I'd say it like this: you don't *decide* your purpose, you *discover* it. Now that's not to say that if you decided you wanted to be rich and famous and worked incessantly towards that goal that you wouldn't achieve it. Probably you would! But it would not necessarily give purpose to life: which is why so many of the rich and famous are so desperately unhappy. Now please don't misunderstand me; finding purpose can and often does provide material wealth and success and that's great. But if your sole ambition is to find the riches and success rather than find your purpose, then you may never be happy!

I believe that each and every one of us has a purpose, a reason for our being here. The Bible states:

> "For I know the plans I have for you," declares the Lord, "plans to prosper you and not to harm you, plans to give you hope and a future." (Jeremiah 29:11)

Elsewhere the Bible also declares:

> "For we are God's workmanship, created in Christ Jesus to do good works, which God prepared in advance for us to do." (Ephesians 2:10)

We need to discover what those plans and 'good works' are, because in them we find our true purpose. However, remember also that we have a free will, so our purpose is not something that is forced upon us like a command from a dictator!

Many years ago, the US Supreme Court Justice, Oliver Wendell Holmes Jr, was on board a train, deep in thought as he studied a legal matter which was shortly due to be heard in court. After a short while the ticket inspector approached and asked the judge for his ticket. Holmes, who was widely known as being somewhat forgetful, searched his belongings inside and out but failed to come up with the ticket or the adequate means of purchasing one. The inspector then recognised his famous passenger and to save any further embarrassment, suggested that the absent-minded judge hand in his ticket or the correct fare on his return journey. Holmes, still perplexed, replied, "Thank you inspector, but the real issue here, and my cause for embarrassment, is not so much a question of the fare but rather, where am I going?"

That's a question a lot of people ask themselves. Where am I going? What do I really want out of life? What should I be doing? In 1864 Lewis Carroll wrote the classic book, *Alice's Adventures in Wonderland.* In the more recent Disney film based on the book, the following dialogue takes place between Alice and the Cheshire cat.

> **Alice:** "I just wanted to ask you which way I ought to go?"
> **Cheshire Cat:** "Well, that depends on where you want to get to."
> **Alice:** "Oh, it really doesn't matter as long as ... "
> **Cheshire Cat:** "Then it really doesn't matter which way you go!"

Many, many people ask themselves that same question, "Which way should I go?" And that's the very question that we shall now try to answer together.

Do you remember another movie, *Back to the Future*, directed by Steven Spielberg? The 'back to the future' idea is a great starting point for discovering your purpose and discerning the direction in which you should travel. Go back in time to when you were a child and you will uncover clues that will point you in the right direction for the future. When you really look, it's not difficult to find purpose; the difficult part usually comes in accepting it when you do find it, and then getting into action and working towards accomplishing it! To put it bluntly, finding your purpose isn't always hard but fulfilling it often is! To find purpose and new direction in life, try asking yourself these questions:

Q. As a child, what were your favourite subjects at school? What did you love to do, where did you achieve the best results and the most recognition?

Q. What were your interests as a child? What are they now? What do you really enjoy doing? What is it that gives you a buzz? What is it that you're good at and enjoy doing so much that you'd gladly do it for free, if you had to? One woman's answer to this question was 'cooking'. What she really loved to do was cook. She looked for ways of applying her passion and in the process she found her purpose and direction in life. Now, a few years later, she makes a very good living from cooking and not only has she written several best-selling books but she also has her own television series. Her name is Delia Smith. Ask yourself the same question, what is it you love to do?

Q. How could this talent or skill be of service or value or use to others? How could you supply a need or create a desire for what it is you are good at?

Q. Now ask yourself this question: What would you do with your life, if you had an absolute copper-bottom guarantee that you couldn't fail? If there were no restrictions whatsoever and there were no obstacles such as money or time, if you absolutely knew that you couldn't fail, what would you attempt to do? When you have answered this question, figure out exactly what you would have to do and what obstacles you would have to overcome in order to achieve this goal. Now you have a purpose, a mission. The question is, will you allow the fear of failure to stop you from fulfilling your mission?

We, each of us, have been blessed with certain gifts, skills, abilities and natural talents. Find out or rediscover what yours are! And don't worry about what you haven't got – just concentrate on what you have got. The following story illustrates this point well.

There was once a poor and illiterate young Greek who applied for a job as cleaner-cum-caretaker for a company in Athens. Being an amiable young man he soon found himself on a shortlist with just one other person. For a time he was the favourite to get the job but he lost out when it was discovered that he couldn't read or write. Completely demoralised by the experience and wanting to run as far away as possible, the young man managed to secure working passage on board a ship bound for England. Picking up the story many years later, the now rich and successful Greek shipping tycoon was being interviewed by a reporter. At the end of the interview the reporter suggested that the businessman should write an autobiography but the tycoon replied, "I'm afraid that wouldn't be possible. You see, I cannot read or write!" The reporter was dumbfounded and responded, "If that's true, then just imagine how much more you would have achieved if you could." The tycoon shook his head. "If I could read and write," he retorted, "I'd have been a caretaker in Athens!"

Let me say it again, we all have gifts, skills, abilities and natural talents. Identify what yours are and don't worry about what you don't have.

Looking at the past and answering the above questions will help you to discover – or rediscover – what your gifts and skills are. Once you have identified them, you will have a good indication of what it is that you should be doing. Let me put it this way: when you utilise your gifts you will, in all likelihood, discover your true purpose.

When I look back to my own school days, my favourite subjects were English language and literature. I was also a natural organiser and many of my classmates and school friends looked to me for leadership. (Either that or I was very bossy!) I was also a persuasive speaker and I often found myself acting as class spokesman. It's hardly surprising, then, to learn that as an adult I have enjoyed a successful career in sales, in business and now as a writer, trainer and motivational speaker. Definitely, all of the dominant characteristics and skills that appeared in me at an early age have remained with me in adult life.

Recently, I watched a documentary on television titled *42 Up* which reinforced this principle. The programme studied and compared the lives of several people, both male and female, who were now all aged 42. The programme, however, began some 35 years previously when the interviewees were all seven-year-old children. Every seven years since the original programme, the producers had gone back and filmed the same people, and this was now the sixth such documentary. I found it compelling viewing. The amazing thing was, almost every one of the people interviewed were either now doing or had been doing the things that they themselves had predicted at the ages of 7 or 14 years old. For example, footage from an earlier programme showed one seven-year-old boy had said he wanted to be a jockey. When the interviewer asked what he thought he might do if he failed as a jockey, the boy thought hard and replied that he would probably become a London cabby. (The children had been asked to consider the questions carefully and so this was not an off-the-cuff response, which is often the case when children say they want to be astronauts or firemen or hairdressers, etc. It was also interesting to note that even at seven years of age, this boy was already showing an active interest in horses. And by the age of 14 he was actually working in a stable yard after school and at the weekends.) Needless to say, this boy became a professional jockey. He did not, however, enjoy much success at riding horses and at 42 years of age, guess what he was doing? That's right, he was driving a black cab in London and loving every minute of it! There were many other examples of self-prophecy fulfilled, right down to would-be mothers who had predicted having three children, to others who had predicted becoming lawyers, and even one child who had predicted becoming a reporter, much the same as the fellow who was interviewing him!

Let me say it again: go back to the future. Go back in time to when you were a child and you will uncover clues that will point you in the right direction for the future.

As I have already said, you don't decide your purpose, you discover it. That's the easy part! The hard part, for some people at least, is then accepting it and getting into action. Beverly Sills, the well-known American opera singer, once stated:

"There are no shortcuts to any place worth going to."

There are no shortcuts to achieving worthwhile goals and life doesn't all of a sudden become a bed of roses once you have decided what it is that you are meant to do. Quite the opposite, in fact! Once you have defined your purpose, that's when the hard work really starts. There will be pain and tears, no doubt, but through it all there will be a sense of satisfaction and enjoyment. In a nutshell, it might be hard work but if you experience a sense of peace, and overwhelming gratitude for what you are doing, then you know you're on the right track.

Of course some people say, "But I don't have any gifts. I'm not skilled in any particular field and I don't have any specific talents that are worth mentioning. God surely must have forgotten about me when he was handing out the personal talents and gifts in life." This is what Zig Ziglar calls the PLOM syndrome: Poor Little Old Me! I can remember one Christmas, as a boy, suffering from the PLOM syndrome and thinking that I had been forgotten about. Listen to the story:

On Christmas morning my parents came downstairs and began handing out the gifts from under the tree. One for my brother, Tony, one for Steve, one for Chris, another one for Tony, one for Mum, another one for Chris and so it went on, as the pile of presents under the tree diminished rapidly. It seemed that everyone else had something, some even had two or three, but there was nothing for me. In actual fact, my parents had been saving the best gift, my present, until last. When they saw me becoming more and more despondent, the ceremony around the tree was put on hold and I was taken by the hand to the garage where my gift, the biggest of them all, was waiting for me. My very first bicycle!

The fact is everyone has gifts. Everyone. If you think you have been overlooked, then think again. Often, our gifts are there all the time: hidden perhaps, dormant maybe, but nevertheless they are there. Often it seems the case that the longer the search and the longer the wait, the bigger the gift is when you do finally discover it. The ability to persevere is, in itself, a gift, and one that is very necessary in order to succeed in any worthwhile endeavour.

Just because a person is not gifted in certain areas, maybe they're not particularly academic or artistic, doesn't mean to say that they are not gifted at all. We have a gifted postman, called Rick. Rick simply delivers the mail but he loves his job and you can tell. He whistles as he rides his bike and he is always smiling and waving or stopping for a friendly chat. He's like a ray of sunshine and brings a lot of happiness into people's lives, including mine.

Martin Luther King put it best when he said:

> "If a man is called to be a street sweeper, he should sweep streets even as Michelangelo painted, or Beethoven composed music, or Shakespeare wrote poetry. He should sweep streets so well that all the hosts of heaven and earth will pause to say, here lived a great street sweeper who did his job well."

If we utilise our gifts and skills as best we can and whenever we can, we will live a meaningful life. The following poem, titled *Be the Best*, by Douglas Malloch, reinforces this message.

Be the Best

If you can't be a pine on the top of the hill,
Be a scrub in the valley, but be
The best little scrub by the side of the rill,
Be a bush if you can't be a tree.
If you can't be a bush, be a bit of grass,
And some highway happier make;
If you can't be a muskie, then be a bass,
But be the liveliest bass in the lake!
We can't all be captains; we've got to be crew,
There's something for all of us here.
There's big work to do and there's lesser to do
And the task we must do is the near.
If you can't be a highway, then just be a trail,
If you can't be the sun, be a star,
It isn't by size that you win or fail.
Just be the best of whatever you are!

Douglas Malloch

I want to move on now to the second objective of this chapter, to impress upon you the need to make plans. I'm talking here about having order, I'm talking about having a method, being organised, having detailed plans – in other words, goals.

You only have to look at nature to see that for successful growth there has to be order. If you look at a pinecone, or you cut an apple in half, or look at a birds nest, or see the symmetry of a flower: all these things bear witness to the fact that successful growth requires organisation, order. The same principle applies with people. If you want your business to grow, and indeed if you seek personal growth, then you also need to have an organised method, a plan of action – in a word, *order*.

There is an old African proverb, known as *The Four Steps to Achievement*, which goes like this:

Plan purposefully. Prepare prayerfully. Proceed positively.
Pursue persistently.

But, of course, it's impossible to effectively prepare, proceed or pursue without taking that first step, to plan purposefully.

It has always amazed me that so few people have personal goals. Now, I'm not talking about ambitions or hopes or dreams, everyone has those. What I'm talking about is having a procedure to follow. What I'm talking about is knowing where you are going and what you must do in order to reach your objective. What I'm talking about is having clearly defined, written down goals.

Very few individuals bother to sit down and plan how to achieve their aspirations. In fact, most people spend more time planning a meeting at work or their Christmas present list or their next holiday than they do planning their lives. Is it such a wonder then, that success and happiness are so elusive? My sentiments are this: if you're not serious enough to plan properly or you can't be bothered to set targets and structured goals, then you're not serious enough to achieve them. My question to some people is, how can a person hit a target if they can't see it, if they are wearing a blindfold? And the answer, of course, is they can't! In order to hit a target or reach a goal the person has to set one in the first place. Success doesn't simply spring up from the middle of nowhere in particular, it doesn't just happen: rather it has to be planned for and worked at.

I have already written in some detail about the techniques of goal-setting in *Maximise Your Potential*. Nevertheless, I want to mention again here, some of the most important guidelines to what is, without doubt, the best kept secret in the world. Let me summarise it for you in one sentence: A goal that is genuinely desired and properly set is already halfway reached. Here, then, are the rules for goal setting and achieving.

1. Commit your plans to paper

This gives your goal substance and clarity but it also gives you something to focus on and serves as a constant reminder to keep you on track. Write your goals out on a piece of paper or card (keep it simple), and put it where you can see them and read them everyday (mine are beside my desk). Remember this: as soon as you think it, ink it! When it comes to goal-setting, a verbal contract is simply not worth the paper it's written on. Your first commitment then, is to commit your goals to paper. Someone once said, "The weakest ink is better than the strongest memory." That's true, so write out your goals, read them daily, and then adopt this code made up from the first seven letters of the alphabet: **A**lways **B**e **C**oncentrating, **D**oing and **E**ndeavouring to **F**ulfil your **G**oals.

2. A goal is something you must be passionate about

It's no use simply making a wish list and then putting it to the back of a drawer to be forgotten about. A goal must be something you will work for, something that's important to you, something that you can focus on and are passionate about.

Have you ever seen a cat watching a mouse hole? Now there's a feline passionate for its cause. The cat is practically oblivious to everything but its target and it will wait patiently for as long as necessary to pursue its prey. I've known our own cat, Rowley, to sit over a mouse hole in our garden (we have a large garden) on and off for three days until he achieved his goal, which he then proudly presented to me! Rowley most definitely has a passion for catching mice and he is continually focused on his goal.

Someone else who had a passion for mice was Walt Disney. Walt Disney was a man who had vision and believed in goals, although he used to joke and say to people, "This whole thing began with a mouse." (A mouse, a vision and a goal.) By the time Disney World in Florida was ready to open its doors to the public, Walt Disney had already died. His wife was invited to say a few words at the opening ceremony. On the big day, the speaker said to her, "I wish that Walt could have seen this." In response Mrs Disney simply said, "He did."

Find something that you can be passionate about, something worthwhile, and something that is bigger than you are. Then set your sights on the target and prepare for battle!

3. Be optimistic, but also rational

Think big and dream big dreams; make your goals worthwhile. Author, James Allen, wrote:

> "The greatest achievement was at first and for a time a dream. The oak sleeps in the acorn; the bird waits in the egg; and in the highest vision of the soul a waking angel stirs. Dreams are the seedlings of realities."

You should aim high and reach for the stars. At least if you miss, you might still hit the moon.

Be optimistic but at the same time be rational. It's fine to dream of becoming an Olympic athlete but not, maybe, if you're approaching retirement! A good goal should push you; it should be something that you have to strive for, but it must also be something that is attainable.

4. Be specific

Once you have set your goal, you should then break it down into little pieces. It's like eating a steak: if you try to swallow it whole you'll most likely choke on it, but when you cut it up into small pieces you can devour it easily. It's the same with goal-setting. Grab hold of a giant-sized goal by all means, but don't bite off more than you can chew at any one time. For example, if you wanted to diet and lose, say, 12 kilograms in weight, you'd stand a far better chance of (sustained) success by setting a specific goal in bite-sized chunks, rather than going on a crash diet and practically starving yourself to death. Remember, it's discipline, drive and determination that determines success, not a one-time, one-off, all out effort!

5. Monitor, review and adjust if necessary

I read recently that a dove has no peripheral vision. It cannot see left or right but only straight ahead. Now this doesn't present a problem when the dove is in flight but when the bird is on the ground feeding, it has to constantly turn its head to monitor the surrounding situation in order to protect itself from danger. Likewise with your goals. You need to constantly monitor, review and adjust your performance if you are to avoid failure.

John C. Maxwell wrote, "A goal is a dream with a deadline." There has to be a plan of action or a timetable to follow, otherwise there is no order to the goal, and instead it is just a mishmash of events or a stab in the dark; a hit and miss campaign. Every author knows that without a goal, without a detailed plan of action or specific guidelines to follow, there is no book. There has to be a plan but, of course, that doesn't mean to say that you can't deviate from the plan. In fact, quite the opposite is true.

When you examine a ship's navigational chart, you'll see that the course from one place to another is originally plotted on the chart as a straight line. The destination is the goal and the straight line, which represents the planned route, is the procedure to follow in order to achieve the goal. However, as soon as the ship sets sail the pilot monitors the ship's progress and the chart begins to take on a completely different look, with a series of zigzags crossing the original straight line. These zigzags, or deviations from the planned route, represent the adjustments that the ship's navigator had to make in order to counteract outside influences, such as wind, currents, and boats or other obstacles in its path which force the ship off its original course. At the end of the day, the destination doesn't change but the journey to achieving it does. Similarly, you should retain your goal but constantly monitor, review and adjust your performance and procedures.

If you review your goals regularly, then you will always be aware of 'where you're at' and what action you need to take. Sometimes you might find that you are getting miles off target or you may even consider that you are no longer on the right track! When this happens you need to understand and remember that it's one thing being persistent and another being pig-headed and obstinate. There is nothing at all wrong with changing course or even changing the destination, if all the indicators point in that direction. Indeed, sometimes it's the wisest thing to do, as the following story illustrates.

One night, prior to the Second World War and just before the invention of radar, a battleship spotted an intermittent light fast approaching from out of the darkness. The captain of the battleship, alarmed but ready for action, ordered his signalman to flash a message in Morse code. "Unidentified vessel change your course immediately." No sooner had the message been dispatched than back came the reply. "Unidentified vessel change *your* course immediately." The captain saw red and instructed his signalman to send a new message: "Change your course immediately, I am a Captain." The response was again instantaneous and read, "Change your course immediately, I am a Seaman, Third Class!" By now the captain was furious and so one last time the signal went out, "Change your course immediately, I am a BATTLESHIP." As before the response came back just as swiftly, "Change *your* course immediately, I am a LIGHTHOUSE!"

Let me reiterate that persistence always conquers resistance in any worthwhile endeavour; but if you discern that your endeavour is no longer worthwhile, then pig-headed obstinacy is nothing more than a complete waste of time and energy. As the saying goes, there's no point flogging a dead horse! Remember to monitor, review and adjust your goals as necessary, so that you always know where you are at.

6. *Don't stop at the winning post*

To succeed in the game of life you have to be constantly moving forward, always with a goal in mind. It's like riding a bicycle: if you stop pedalling then sooner or later you'll lose your balance and fall off. It's the same with goal-setting: if you stop setting goals and making plans, then you'll slow down until eventually you stop moving forward. Then you'll lose your balance, fall over into the dirt and run the risk of rusting up! What am I saying? Simply this; don't ever stop making plans or setting new goals. It doesn't matter how old you are. As Mark Twain once said, "Age is mostly a matter of mind. If you don't mind then it doesn't matter!" So *don't ever stop*. Even when you achieve a goal, don't rest on your laurels, don't be satisfied with past achievements; instead set yourself new goals.

The accomplished English long-distance swimmer, Florence Chadwick, was very much a goal-oriented person. Having already conquered the Straits of Gibraltar, Bosporus and Dardanelles, in 1950 she became the first woman to swim the English Channel in both directions! Immediately afterwards she set her sights on a new goal, to replace the one she had just lost by winning it. This new goal, however, would be far more dangerous. Swimming a distance of some 33 kilometres through the shark-infested waters of the Catalina Channel, from Catalina Island to Los Angeles in California.

The attempt was scheduled for the American Independence Day: the 4th of July, 1952. When the day finally arrived Chadwick entered the water at Catalina Island and began swimming towards the California coastline, which, unfortunately, was covered by dense fog. Hour after hour she swam on relentlessly through the icy-cold water. Several times the riflemen in the support boat had to frighten off the sharks. Florence Chadwick was in the water for almost 16 hours before she gave up and asked to be pulled in to the boat. The elements had taken their toll – she was completely exhausted and frozen to the bone – but the thing that had made her quit was the fact that she couldn't see the finishing line. The fog had so obscured her view and so completely demoralised her that it sapped her of the will to go on. Soon after being hauled out of the water, Chadwick was to be demoralised even further when it was discovered that she was less than a kilometre away from shore!

Florence Chadwick was utterly devastated but nevertheless, she immediately set herself a new goal, a fresh target to give her renewed hope and the inspiration to continue. Just two months later she was back again for another attempt. Once again the coastline was covered in dense fog but this time she overcame the obstacle and won through. Not only was she the first ever woman to swim the Catalina Channel, but she also broke the previous all-time speed record by some two hours!

Let me say it once again: to succeed in the game of life you have to be constantly moving forward, always with a goal or target in mind. So don't ever stop setting new targets and making plans. And whenever you succeed and achieve your goals, make sure that you set new ones to replace the ones you just lost by winning them.

We have now looked at ways of discovering your purpose, finding direction and making plans to achieve your purpose. Now putting all that into practice is pretty much up to you, my friend.

In my next letter, we'll take things a step further and look at the dual subjects of finding opportunity and taking risks. Until next time then, I remain once again,

Yours cordially,
Uncle Bob

Chapter Four
Opportunity and Taking Risks

The reason so many people never get anywhere in life is because when opportunity knocks, they are out in the garden looking for four-leafed clovers.
Walter P. Chrysler
(founder of the Chrysler motor company)

Dear _ _ _ _ _ _ _ (fill in your name),

My copy of the Collins English Thesaurus lists the following synonyms for the words *opportunity/opportune*: advantageous, appropriate, chance, convenient, favourable, fortunate, lucky break, suitable opening and well-timed. Sounds wonderful, doesn't it? People say, "I'm just waiting for the right opportunity." In fact, everyone is seeking opportunity of one kind or another. Wouldn't it be great if you could wake up tomorrow morning, open your front door and find opportunity sitting there waiting for you on the doorstep, in much the same way as you can open up a dictionary and find the word *opportunity* waiting for you amongst the pages?

Sometimes it does happen like that! I've read that Bob Hoskins began his career as an actor quite by accident. It's reported that Hoskins was in a theatre in the West End of London, and was having a drink at the bar while he waited for a friend who was building some stage scenery for a forthcoming production. As he sat at the bar a man came up to him and said, "Okay, it's your turn." Hoskins, somewhat puzzled, looked up and replied, "Sorry?" The man answered, "You're up next. Follow me." "For what?" said

Hoskins. "For the audition of course, that's what you're here for isn't it?" Hoskins smiled to himself and, staying quiet about the real reason for his being there, he played along and took part in the audition. The producers were so impressed with his ability that they offered Bob Hoskins the leading role in the play! And so began a very distinguished career.

Fortunate? Good luck? A case of being in the right place at the right time? Certainly such things do happen, from time to time. However, they only occur very infrequently and then mostly only when they are completely unexpected! There is no point at all, therefore, sitting around and waiting for the right time and right place to simply happen for you. Rather, you must get up and get going and discover the right time and the right place for yourself. There's an old adage that puts it very well:

The right time and the right place is usually, right now!

For a lot of people, it seems that opportunity can be the most elusive event in the world. Indeed, I would agree that opportunity *is* elusive! By that, I don't mean to say that it never happens. In fact, the very opposite is true. Opportunity is always happening all around us, it is literally everywhere. But it is elusive in that, generally speaking, it is in disguise!

Our human nature is to want opportunity to be plainly recognisable and for 'it' to be handed to us on a plate. We want things to be easy, not difficult; we want things to be comfortable, not unpleasant; we want things to be safe and sure, not risky or uncertain. Thomas Edison once said: "There is much more opportunity than there are people to see it." What Edison was saying is that there is always abundant opportunity; it's just that people don't see it. Either that, or else they don't want to see it, not really! You see, whenever an opportunity presents itself there is a decision to be made. Do we grab the opportunity and run with it – do we jump into action and risk failure, ridicule and defeat? Or do we put it off and wait for a more 'opportune' moment or until things become a little clearer or somehow more certain?

Doing nothing is, of course, the easier option: no risk, discomfort or unpleasantness there! Seizing the opportunity and running with it, on the other hand, is far harder and more painful but, as the saying goes, "No pain, no gain!"

So how does a person actually find opportunity? It's all very well saying that opportunity lies all around us, but what does it really look like? I'll let Orison Swett Marden (1848–1924), author and one-time editor of the popular American magazine, *Success,* answer that question.

> "The golden opportunity you are seeking is in yourself. It is not in your environment, it is not in luck or chance, or in the help of others, it is in yourself alone."

Opportunity lies hidden within you right now and at the same time – although it may seem invisible – it is also all around you, just waiting to be discovered.

Understand that "opportunity doesn't knock on doors, it hides behind them!" So then, don't wait around for opportunity to knock on your door, instead start opening up a few doors (go with your ideas) and surprise yourself! What am I saying? Well, let me put it like this: if I were to be more specific about you and your individual circumstances I'd probably be saying something along the lines of, "Answer that advertisement; make that telephone call; visit that prospect; apply for that job; write that letter; enrol for that course; enter that race or ask whoever it is for whatever it is that you want." Do you understand what I'm getting at? Just in case you don't, let me borrow the words of author, Bob Gass, and say:

> "The door of opportunity is always marked *PUSH.*"

Here's another proverbial saying with the same meaning:

> God gives every bird its food, but he doesn't throw it in the nest.

George Bernard Shaw was more blunt when he said:

> "The people who get on in this world are the people who get up and look for the circumstances they want, and, if they can't find them, make them."

Here are a couple of suggestions for you. Hopefully, they will challenge your thinking and help you find the 'right' opportunities or at the very least make a start.

Possibility Thinking

Dr Robert H. Schuller is a man who knows all about finding opportunities and capitalising on them. Dr Schuller is the founder, and at the time of writing senior pastor, of the Crystal Cathedral in Garden Grove, California, USA. The cathedral is an amazing structure: costing more than $US15 million to build, it is constructed almost entirely out of glass! (hence the name). When Schuller began this massive project he had no money and absolutely no means, or so he thought, of obtaining any. All he had was a vision, an idea! However, Dr Schuller understood that opportunities are born from ideas and in his best-selling book, *Tough Times Never Last but Tough People Do!* he describes how he was able to raise enough money to build the cathedral. I'll leave you to read his book to find out how, but suffice for me to say here, that Dr Schuller's secret to finding the 'right' opportunities, (i.e. the cash to finance his project) comes down to what he calls Possibility Thinking.

In a nutshell, Possibility Thinking works like this: when an ideal or an idea is born, you take a piece of paper and write down the numbers one to ten. Then, put on your thinking hat and list ten possible ways to achieve your objective. It doesn't matter how far-fetched the idea might at first appear to be – if it's at all feasible, write it down. On Dr Schuller's original list were ideas such as asking people or companies for $1 million donations and selling each window, (there are 10,866 of them) at $500 a window.

Possibility Thinking is simply thinking up a list of conceivable ways of obtaining your objective. Try it out for yourself. Whatever it is that you want to do or become or achieve, list ten ideas that could possibly help you accomplish your objective. These ideas are then ten opportunities staring you straight in the face. The question now is will you grasp the opportunities and run with them or will you put the list to the back of a drawer somewhere and wait around again, for a more suitable time? Understand this, life waits for no one, and neither does opportunity. Finding opportunities is like harvesting potatoes; they don't just *turn up* by themselves, they have to *be turned up!* Once you have drawn up your list of possibilities you then need to get into action, you need to seize the day or 'carpe diem' because nobody else is going to do it for you.

Brainstorming

Following on from the above, brainstorming is a similar technique but one that is more suitable for a corporate or family environment, i.e. when there is more than one person involved. The idea here is to pool resources, with the philosophy being that many minds working on a problem are better than one.

To conduct an effective brainstorming exercise you need to elect a chairperson, to control the session, to keep it on track and stop people from arguing, debating or wandering off onto another subject. The chairperson must give the participants an objective, something that they are trying to accomplish. A time limit should be set – 20 minutes is a good time – and everyone should then voice as many different ideas as they can come up with – no restrictions. The chairperson encourages the participants to come up with more and more ideas and then simply writes everything down – no matter how far-fetched!

It is very important that none of these ideas are challenged during the time set for the brainstorming session, regardless of how trivial or foolish an idea might sound. This is something that must be made very clear in the beginning. The objective of the exercise is to stimulate creative inspiration. It just might be the case that one person thinks of three or four silly ideas, but then comes up with a real gem! If that person is challenged or criticised for the silly ideas during the open session there is a strong likelihood that he or she will clam up for fear of being ridiculed or having ideas rejected. Then the gem of an idea would never get voiced at all!

As with Possibility Thinking, the result of a successful brainstorming session will be a list of possibilities. These ideas can then be sifted and sorted into a list of the more credible. These make up another powerful set of golden opportunities just waiting to be taken up. The question again is will you now grasp them and run with them or will you put the list to the back of your mind and wait around for a 'better' or more 'appropriate' time?

Opportunity *is* all around us just waiting to be discovered. But capitalising on an opportunity lies in the doing, not in the waiting around. To paraphrase a well-known children's nursery rhyme: there were two little dickie birds sat upon a wall – one decided to fly off. How many were left? Mostly, people answer one, but the correct answer is still two. Just because one bird decided to fly off doesn't mean that it actually did fly off! Likewise, it's one thing deciding to take action and it's another actually doing it. So then, don't sit around waiting for opportunity to come to you because opportunity is doing the exact same thing. Opportunity is waiting for you to come to it!

The words of the old Greek proverb say it well:

> The fox that waited for the chickens to fall off the perch died of hunger.

That's the same as saying, if your get up and go has got up and gone then get up and go after it!

Napoleon Hill, author of the best-selling book, *Think And Grow Rich*, wrote:

> "Do not wait. The time will never be just right. Start where you stand, and work with whatever tools you may have at your command, and better tools will be found as you go along."

This, again, is another way of saying 'carpe diem' (seize the day). Napoleon Hill goes on to say:

> "Procrastination is the bad habit of putting off until the day after tomorrow what should have been done the day before yesterday."

So, why is it that people so frequently procrastinate? Why do they put off making a decision or taking action? The answer, very simply, is because of the risk involved. As I have said already, there is a human tendency to want opportunity to be plainly recognisable and for everything to be handed to us on a plate. We like things to be easy, not difficult; we want things to be comfortable, not unpleasant; we prefer certainty to risky. Making a decision or taking the plunge usually involves some element of risk and this, of course, is uncomfortable. Rather than taking the risk, many people would prefer to postpone or put off acting upon a decision until some later date. In so doing, they rationalise their inactivity by thinking that at least if they wait they retain a *hope* that things will turn out all right in the end. Seizing the day means that you run the risk of failure, defeat, rejection and losing whatever hopes and dreams you may have had to start off with. Unfortunately, there is no easy route. If you want to discover new horizons you have to have the courage to lose sight of the shore. You have to set sail. And what if you haven't got a boat? Well, don't just sit around waiting for your ship to come in, instead swim out and find it!

Entrepreneur, Sir Richard Branson, founder of the Virgin group of companies, is a man who seems to have an uncanny knack for spotting the 'right opportunities'. He is also a man who knows that in order to win you must first of all enter the race. And that, of course, means that you run the risk of losing. If you read Branson's autobiography, *Losing My Virginity,* you'll see that his life has been a constant risk-taking adventure. A prominent example of this is in the setting up of the airline, Virgin Atlantic, back in 1984.

At that time the collapse of Laker Airlines (in the UK), was still fresh in the minds of the media, the financial markets and the general public at large. Everyone thought that Branson was out of his mind getting involved in an industry that he had no experience in and taking on the bigger airlines. It was, after all, competition from the 'big boys' that put Laker Airlines out of business!

Branson, however, had done his homework and saw a golden opportunity to capitalise on the mistakes made by Laker Airlines. Of course, as with all opportunity, there was an element of risk but Branson has learnt how to spread the risk and so diminish the threat of losing. The following is an excerpt taken from a paper on entrepreneurship written by Richard Branson.

"I'd paid close attention to the mistakes which appeared to have caused the [Laker] failure, as well as what might be done to avoid repeating them. We would obviously need to protect ourselves against currency fluctuations. We should go for carrying freight as well as passengers, and that would mean using 747s instead of DC10s. By concentrating too exclusively on offering a discount price-led service, Laker had made themselves vulnerable to price-cutting by the bigger carriers. And by the time Laker introduced a business class – two months before the collapse – it was too late.

So we decided to have a unique and high quality business class right from the start, to complement a competitive and good economy class. It wasn't just that it had the potential to pay for lower fares in economy class – which in fact is what happened. It also meant we'd have a regular clientele who wouldn't desert us at the first hint of a skirmish in the price war.

Years later, lessons learnt from the misfortunes of others have paid off. Upper Class, Virgin Atlantic's business class, has won a string of awards from the travel press. And it's so heavily booked on some routes that it is expanded way beyond the upstairs cabin to occupy half the space on the plane."

(I have travelled in Upper Class on Virgin Atlantic and so I can vouch for the above statement. It really is a unique and high quality service.)

Like all successful people, Richard Branson looks for opportunities and when he sees one he seizes it. He knows that it will involve risk and so he looks for ways to minimise the odds of failing. That's a good philosophy for us all to follow.

I have my own technique for minimising risk. Simply stated it is to always have an alternative strategy or a fall-back position. In other words, whenever there is a major decision or choice to be made, whenever something has to be negotiated or there is a deal on the table – whenever there is a situation that involves taking a risk – I find it much easier to deal with if there is a Plan B to fall back on, just in case things don't work out with Plan A. I want to recommend that you adopt this same strategy to minimise risk in your own life.

Here's an example of how the alternative strategy technique might work for you.

Suppose you are offered two different jobs but you don't know which to accept. The dilemma is that in accepting one position you automatically reject the other, which will then be offered to someone else. What do you do? How do you make the right decision? Well, the long and the short of it is simply this, there is no way to really know. You just have to go along with your gut feeling and take a risk. That risk will be so much easier to take, however, if you have a Plan B (and even a Plan C and D) to revert to if things don't work out. When you have a fall-back position you are able to deal with, decide upon or negotiate from strength because, although the decision may still involve risk, it is not as though everything is completely dependent upon one roll of the dice. You still have other options and alternatives you can consider if you need to. Let me put it like this: having a Plan B enables you to act like a duck. You can appear to be all calm, collected and unruffled on the surface, even if you're paddling like mad underneath!

Another way of minimising potential risk is to simply ask yourself, what's the worst possible thing that can happen. If the answer to that question is something you can live with, then the risk (providing it's a worthwhile venture) is probably worth taking.

In the final analysis, if the worst thing that can happen is tolerable, then the risk is minimal and you should do it.

Risk is all about taking chances. There is no such thing as a 'sure thing,' not with anything worthwhile at any rate! Opportunities and risk go together hand in glove. You simply cannot have one without the other. Think about it. A life void of risk is a life void of opportunity and what kind of life is that? I once read a cynical but somewhat amusing poem on a poster titled, *Anti-Risk Campaign*, the connotations of which, are very obvious. Here it is.

> Don't look; you might see.
> Don't listen; you might hear.
> Don't think; you might learn.
> Don't walk; you might stumble.
> Don't run; you might fall.
> Don't decide; you might be wrong.
> Don't risk; you might fail.
> Don't live; you might die.

Remaining with the theme of whether or not to take risks, here's a tale to demonstrate the point. There were two seeds lying side by side in the farmyard soil. The first little seed wanted to grow big and strong and produce fruit and seed of its own. So the little seed sent roots deep into the earth where it was able to find all the water and nutrients that it would need. At the same time, the root system was able to provide an anchor to give the seedling, then the sapling and finally the tree, the stability it needed to sustain its growth. The seed wanted to stretch its limbs towards the sky, to feel the sun's caressing rays upon its foliage and to provide abundant fruit that would be enjoyed by many.

This first little seed had lofty ambitions and so it grew and became the beautiful tree that it had always dreamed of being.

The second little seed wanted the same things, but the second little seed was afraid. The soil was cold and dark and uninviting. The seed was afraid that if it sent its roots down into the earth, it might encounter rocks, or even worse, a worm! (Worms, of course, are very partial to tender roots!) And what if it should sprout; surely the delicate sprouts would be damaged trying to push through the heavy compacted soil above it. And if, perchance, the shoots did manage to make it to the surface, wouldn't they be trampled underfoot, or scorched by the burning sun or strangled by the other plants all vying for the same space?

The second little seed decided it was too risky! It would wait and see what happened to the other seeds first. Besides which, the seed was quite comfortable where it was. For the time being, at least, the second little seed decided to play it safe and remain dormant. Unfortunately, however, that very same morning a farmyard hen scratching about in the undergrowth discovered the waiting seed and promptly ate it!

Now the message behind this old fable is simple: those who choose not to take risks often get eaten up with the whys and worries of the world. Don't let that happen to you. Instead, remember, nothing ventured is nothing gained.

Life, itself, is a risk. Think about it. You take a risk every time you get into a car and every time you cross the street. In fact, getting out of bed in the morning is a risk! Did you know that thousands of people are injured each year, just getting out of bed? (Many people fall over, others bang their head, or step on the cat, or trip over some other discarded object or article of clothing, etc.) If you want to really 'live' your life you have to be prepared to make decisions and take risks. Here's a verse that has often inspired me into action when I have been fearful:

> To laugh is to risk appearing the fool.
> To weep is to risk appearing sentimental.
> To reach out for another is to risk involvement.
> To expose your feelings is to risk exposing your true self.
> To place your ideas and your dreams before a crowd is to
> risk their loss.
> To love is to risk not being loved in return.
> To live is to risk dying.
> To try is to risk failure.
> To ask is to risk rejection.
> But risks must be taken,
> because the greatest hazard in life is to risk nothing.
> The person who risks nothing does nothing, has nothing
> and is nothing.
> He may avoid suffering and sorrow, but he cannot learn,
> feel, change, grow, love or live his certitudes.
> He is a slave; he has forfeited his freedom.
> Only a person who risks is really free.

When it comes to seizing opportunity, some people just dream of worthy accomplishments while others stay awake, take the necessary risks and achieve them.

David Sarnoff (1891–1971) was a Russian immigrant to the United States, the so-called land of opportunity. He once said,

> "There is plenty of security in the cemetery; what I long for is opportunity."

David Sarnoff found his own opportunity and seized it. He went to work for the Marconi Company, founded by Guglielmo Marconi, the Italian physicist who invented the radio, back in 1896. For 20 years, until 1916, radio had only ever been used as a means of communicating messages to and fro, but David Sarnoff discovered its true potential. He went on to become the pioneer behind commercial radio broadcasting directly into people's homes. The music that we listen to on our radios today is available to us simply because one man saw an opportunity and ran with it.

Remember, opportunity is all around us; it is literally everywhere, just waiting to be discovered. Seek out fresh opportunity for yourself; push a few doors and see what's behind them. Create a Possibility Thinking list or organise a brainstorming session but whatever you do, do it now. Listen to your inner voice right now, the one that's saying, "I should do this ... I must ... I can ... I will." Capture this inspiration, hold on to it and don't let go. Make yourself a promise to get into action; write out your plan of action and sign it as your word, your bond, your solemn promise to do something about it; to seize the opportunity and take whatever risk needs to be taken.

The greatest obstacle you will face when seizing opportunities and taking the necessary risks to achieve success is, of course, fear of failure. This, then, will be the topic of my next letter but for now, I remain as always,

Yours cordially,
Uncle Bob

Chapter Five

Overcoming Fear and Indecision

It doesn't matter which side of the fence you get off on sometimes. What matters most is getting off! You cannot make progress without making decisions.
Jim Rohn (speaker, trainer and writer)

Dear _ _ _ _ _ _ _ (fill in your name),

It's been said that ships moored in the harbour are safe, but that, of course, is not what ships are meant for! Similarly with you. If you are fearful and indecisive, if you keep putting off making a decision or taking action – in other words, if you remain in the harbour and never leave the dock, then you might be safe (for a while at least) but that's not what life is about. Unlike any other animal on the face on the planet, human instinct is to do more than just survive. We are designed to do more than simply eat, drink, sleep, procreate and stay alive. We are built with an inquisitive, adventurous, creative and calculating mind that desires, even commands, that we leave the harbour and venture out on to the high seas in search of progress and betterment. Let me put it like this: a human being is meant to be a 'human doing'. And, of course, to be a human doing means that we have to overcome the fear and indecision that would otherwise hold us back.

In this letter then, we shall be looking at fear and indecision and discussing ways to overcome these mighty opponents.

First of all though, I want to point out that this subject is not at all complicated. There are two things that you really need to understand about fear. The first is that *everyone* suffers from it in some form or another – at least occasionally, if not often! It's not just you alone! When I say, 'everyone,' I include myself and, in fact, all successful people everywhere, as well as rich people, famous people, presidents, prime ministers and even kings and queens. Let me say it again, everyone experiences fear. Fear of what people might think, fear of failure, fear of rejection, fear of disaster, fear of death, fear of ... you name it and someone, somewhere, at sometime or other is fearful of it! The second thing that you need to understand about fear, is this: the only way to overcome it is to take action and tackle the fear head on, which, more often than not, means having to physically do the thing that you fear doing. And that's, basically, all there is to it: understanding that everyone experiences fear and that the only way to deal with it, is to simply do the thing that you are afraid of! The following tale demonstrates the point rather well:

> Jimmy's mother shouted up the stairs, "Come on, son, it's time to get up and get ready for school." But Jimmy pulled the doona up over his head and ignored his mother's calling. A few minutes later she knocked on his door and in a firmer voice she called, "Come on. You have to get up right now, otherwise you'll be late!" Jimmy replied from under the covers, "I'm not going to school today. In fact, I'm never going again."
>
> "Don't be silly," said his mother, "You've got to go to school."
>
> "I'm NOT going!" was the response. "There are almost 1000 kids in that school and they all hate me, every last one of them. Even the teachers and the caretaker hate me and every day I end up in some sort of fight or conflict. So give me just one good reason why I should go."
>
> "I'll do more than that," said his mother. "I'll give you two: first, because you are 42 years of age, and second, because you are the Principal!"

Now, you may smile but my point behind this story is this: confrontation, or the prospect of confrontation, is sometimes inevitable and often causes fear and indecision. However, trying to run or hide away from it only compounds the problem. As I've said, the only way to overcome fear is to tackle the problem head-on.

Of course, fear does not always play the part of the monster whose mission is to overpower us and keep us from achieving. Sometimes it is the complete opposite. Sometimes fear is a good thing which protects us and keeps us out of harm's way. For example, when the human body experiences fear in the presence of danger, or when it experiences shock (also cold and fatigue) the hormone called adrenaline is produced. This raises the blood pressure and the heartbeat, which then provides the body with more oxygen. Adrenaline also causes the body to create glucose, which provides us with additional energy (so that we can escape or fight!).

Obviously, then, not all fear is bad. I know that if I were in the jungle and came across a hungry tiger, then I would very much want to experience fear, and lots of it! We will not, however, be discussing this type of fear here. Instead, we will concentrate on the kind of personal fear that holds a person back and stops him from achieving his potential.

When prolonged, fear and indecision are debilitating; they sap us of energy and the will to go on. Fear and indecision stop a great many people from achieving, simply because they stop them from ever *attempting* in the first place. The American philosopher, William James, wrote:

> "There is no more miserable human being than one in whom nothing is habitual but indecision."

Think about it, what could you accomplish if you were not in the least bit afraid of trying? That's an awesome thought, is it not? Fear, then, is a major obstacle standing in the way of success, a major obstacle that many don't manage to surmount. And yet, ironically, most of the time our fears are completely unwarranted. In fact, it has been suggested that around 90 per cent of the things we worry about never actually happen. Now, exactly how someone can quantify such a figure is beyond me, but the point itself must be valid. (Insurance companies obviously think so: it's the reason they are so wealthy!)

As human beings we all seem to have a tendency to make mountains out of molehills – at least every once in a while, if not more often! Indeed, it has been said that the greatest cause of ulcers is mountain-climbing over molehills! Often, people allow their fears and doubts to have far too much control over them. It's as though each of us has an independent person inside us or an inner-voice, which is constantly trying to hold us back and stop us from attempting to achieve. As individuals we are, very often, our own worst enemy. This anonymous poem reinforces the point rather dramatically.

> An enemy I had, whose face I stoutly strove to know,
> For hard he dogged my steps unseen, wherever I did go.
> My plans he balked, my aims he foiled, he blocked my onward way.
> When for some lofty goal I toiled, he grimly told me, "Nay."
> One night I seized him and held him fast, from him the veil did draw,
> I looked upon his face at last and lo – myself I saw!

Truly, we are our own worst enemy, or at least, we have the potential of being so. Conversely, however, we also have the potential of being our best ally, friend and supporter. When you understand this truth you begin to see that you, yourself, can be your own greatest hindrance or your own greatest helper. At the end of the day, as the saying goes, the buck stops here – with you. You must decide what you will be, hinderer or helper.

You must also understand that you, and you only, are completely and absolutely responsible for your own happiness. (I am talking here about true happiness which is always coupled with a sense of well-being or peace of mind.) Material things can't make you truly happy, people can't make you truly happy, situations and places and times and events can't make you truly happy. It is only when *you* allow yourself to be happy that you will then *be* happy. Similarly, when it comes to overcoming fear, you, and only you, are the one in the driving seat. You make the choice. You make the decision. You can either be your own worst enemy and allow the fear to control you or, conversely, you can be your own best ally and conquer the fear.

It's not easy! Success is never easy. I once heard it described like this: it's as though we have two dogs inside our head – a good dog and a bad dog – and both of them are constantly fighting for the same piece of meat. What we must do is feed the good dog and starve the bad dog. To explain the analogy, when our (negative) inner voice creates anxiety, doubts and fears by going on and on about why we shouldn't attempt to do this or what would happen if we did that, this is like the bad dog. We must starve the bad dog (get rid of the negative self-talk) by taking way its food. And how do you do this? By feeding the good dog with positive self-talk. In other words, use positive affirmations to replace the negative thoughts and, in so doing, you will overcome or, at least diminish, the fear enough to conquer it.

However, if you listen to the bad dog and allow the fear to take a hold on you, it will try its utmost to overpower you and beat you into submission. Take the example of the small boy walking past a charming old church on a very dark, but otherwise pleasant, evening. When he walked along, lackadaisically, whistling a happy tune he was fine. But then he looked over into the churchyard and noticed the shadows and the gravestones, so he stopped whistling and quickened his pace. After a few strides his fear took hold of him and he suddenly got the urge to run, and as he ran his fear turned to terror – on what was, after all, just a dark, but otherwise pleasant, night! Let me put it like this: if you give in to your fear it will overwhelm you; if you give it an inch it will take a mile. Don't do it. Don't give it an inch. Instead, choose to control your fear and not let it control you.

Here's how one man learnt how to do just that. Mr Meekness (so called by his workmates because of his timid character) was a conscientious hard worker. He was also, however, too fearful to ask his penny-pinching boss for the raises that were due to him.

Then one day Mr Meekness found an envelope full of money – $1,000 in crisp, new $100 notes. His good fortune gave him a sense of security and with new-found courage he marched off to the manager's office to demand what was due to him. He told the manager just what he thought of him and insisted that he got a big raise or else he would quit there and then and go and work somewhere else. The manager, somewhat taken aback, put up a feeble attempt to resist the onslaught but, eventually, he was overcome by Mr Meekness's firmness and the strength of his argument. In the end, justice was done and he received the raise.

Later that same day Mr Meekness went to pay the $1,000 cash into his bank but, when he tried to do so, he discovered that the money was, in fact, counterfeit! Of course, Mr Meekness lost his treasure but in its place he found something far more valuable. He discovered that, forged notes or genuine ones, the thought that he had $1,000 in cash gave him the confidence he needed to overcome his fear. He discovered that positive thoughts and affirmations really *do* make a difference!

As I have already discussed in some detail – in my letter on 'Attitude and Positive Thinking' (Chapter 2) – we, as human beings, have the ability to control our thoughts and our attitudes. We can choose how we will react to any given situation. Understand, then, that it's not so much what happens to you that makes a difference but how you react or deal with what happens to you.

Dr Viktor E. Frankl is a psychiatrist who survived years of deprivation, cruelty and torture by the Nazis in the Second World War. Being Jewish, he endured unspeakable horrors in the Nazi concentration camps of Auschwitz and Dachau, where he both witnessed and was subjected to the most horrifying atrocities. In his best-selling book, *Man's Search For Meaning*, he describes how he managed to survive. It is compelling reading but, for me, the gist of the book can be summarised in this one statement made by Dr Frankl, "The last of the human freedoms is to choose one's attitude in any given set of circumstances." Dr Frankl learnt that during his imprisonment, he could not control his surroundings or the way he was treated, but he could control his reaction to what was happening to him.

Let me say it once again, we can control our thoughts and attitudes. We can determine how we will react.

Bearing this in mind then, whenever you experience doubts, inner fear or trepidation, whenever you find yourself having negative thoughts, you can control them; you can forcibly change the fearful, negative thoughts and swap them for positive ones.

In effect then, the way to overcome your inner fear is to make your positive self-talk so dominant that it completely drowns out your negative self-talk. I can tell you, from experience, that the more you practise this technique the easier it will become. Now, that's not to say that in using positive self-talk you will never again experience fear and indecision, but rather, you will be more in control of it and not the other way around!

As I've mentioned before, a lot of people do not share my sentiments when it comes to positive thinking. In fact, some people actually choose to be negative. For these people everything is doom and gloom and it's almost as if they prefer it that way. It seems they are just not happy unless they have something to moan about. I find that a real shame, but I suppose it takes all sorts of people to make up this world of ours. As William James once put it, "What kind of a world would this world be, if everyone in it were just like me?" The negative thinkers will usually say something along the lines of, "Positive thinking! Not that old chestnut again. Let me tell you, I've tried it all before and it didn't work then and it won't work now!" The irony, of course, is that with these people the philosophy has already worked, but in reverse. You see, they have been starving the good dog and feeding the bad dog for so long, that the bad dog is now huge in comparison to the good dog which has become puny and insignificant. If this has happened to you, if you find yourself being more and more negative, then please listen again, carefully, to the following advice: *start feeding your mind with positive thoughts again and starve the enemy to death.*

Remember, persistence always conquers resistance, eventually. So, keep at it. Don't quit after an hour or a day or a week or a month, but stick with it continually and adopt this practice as a personal way of life. It won't be easy, especially not in the beginning. In fact, it will take discipline, drive and determination to turn your everyday thinking around, but the good news is in doing so you'll start to see positive results happening straight away.

Ralph Waldo Emerson understood the secret of positive thinking and the power of our mind. He wrote:

> "What lies behind us, and what lies before us, pales in
> significance when compared to what lies within us."

Remember, we can control what lies within us, we can control our thinking and our attitudes.

Let me back-pedal for a moment and reiterate that everyone experiences fear. It is a natural phenomenon and there is no way to completely eliminate it, not until we die that is! Instead of trying to eliminate it or run away from it we would all do much better to learn how to control and overcome our fears, especially those which stop us from attempting. Listen to the wise words of William Shakespeare:

> "Our doubts are traitors, and make us lose the good we oft
> might win by fearing to attempt."

Regardless of how simple or easy a task may appear to be, if an element of risk is introduced to the equation then the resultant fear can become a giant hurdle. Take, for example, the often-quoted analogy of 'walking the plank'. Imagine I take a plank of wood, similar in size to a scaffold board, and lay it on the ground. Now I offer you $20 to walk the length of the plank without falling off. Easy enough; no problems there; no risk; no fear; just easy pickings, right? Now, imagine I take that same plank of wood and climb to the top of a 20-storey building. I go out onto the roof and place the plank across the void between this building and a neighbouring one which is a similar height. However, this time I offer you, not $20 but $1,000 (and not in forged $100 notes) to walk the plank! (The same task but a far greater reward.) All of a sudden things take on a whole new perspective don't they? The task might remain the same but now we have introduced an element of risk which produces fear, and which, in this case, would stop all but the most foolhardy from attempting to claim the $1,000 in question. (Incidentally, I forgot to tell you that at 20 storeys high, buildings are designed to sway to and fro as a way of relieving tension. At that height there is also usually a strong prevailing wind – and no safety nets!)

Of course, the above example is a little far-fetched but nevertheless, the point is that fear, in whatever form, stops a great many people from achieving simply because it stops them from ever attempting in the first place.

Another example of this can be found in the Biblical story of David and Goliath. During the reign of King Saul, the Israelites and the Philistines prepared to do battle against each other. The two armies were camped on opposite hills with a valley in between separating them. For 40 days there was an impasse as each side waited for the other to either attack or retreat, and so lose the advantage of fighting from the high ground. And for 40 days, during this impasse, the Philistine champion named Goliath, who was over 270 cm tall, came out of the Philistine camp and went down the valley to challenge the Israelites. (Over 270 cm tall sounds impossible, but in recent history the *Guinness Book of Records* registers Robert Wadlow [1918–1940] as the world's tallest man measuring in at just over 271 cm.) Every morning and every evening Goliath would bellow his challenge across to the Israelite camp, mocking them and daring them to produce their own champion to fight against him and so determine the war's outcome by means of single combat. And for 40 days, whenever the Israelites saw Goliath, the Bible says, they all ran from him in great fear.

But then one day a young shepherd boy, named David, visited the Israelite camp to bring supplies to his elder brothers. He heard Goliath shouting his usual defiant challenge and so David, armed only with his faith, his slingshot and a few pebbles, persuaded the king to let him go out and fight the Philistine giant! And the rest of the story, as they say, is history.

My point, in relating this account, is to demonstrate once again that fear stops a lot of people from ever attempting anything. The only real difference between the shepherd boy, David, and the rest of the Israelite army was one of faith or attitude. The Israelite soldiers thought Goliath was so big that no one would be able to overcome him. David thought Goliath was so big that he would never be able to miss him! Similarly with us, when it comes to overcoming fear and indecision the difference between success and failure, between striving forwards or stagnating, is our attitude, drive and determination and, if we are like David, our faith! The shepherd boy, David, went on to become King of Israel. He also wrote many of the psalms contained in the Bible, of which one of the most famous is Psalm 23, "The Lord is my shepherd." In this psalm David wrote, "Even though I walk through the valley of the shadow of death, I will fear no evil, for you [God] are with me." (Brackets mine.)

When it comes to overcoming fear and indecision I have personally found that there is nothing in this world as powerful as prayer. Now I fully understand and appreciate that not everyone will support my Christian beliefs but, as I am writing on this subject, I want to share with you how I overcome my times of major indecisiveness. In a word, the answer is *prayer.*

You know, when Jesus taught his disciples how to pray he said to them, "Ask and it will be given to you; seek and you will find; knock and the door will be opened to you." (Luke 11:9) If you haven't already done so, I want to recommend you try it yourself.

Now, I want to change direction slightly and briefly touch upon another topic that is often the cause of much fear and indecision – change.

Change, or the threat of it, often produces apprehension, worry, anxiety, doubt and uncertainty. Change also causes fear. Fear for one's safety or welfare, fear of the unknown, fear of making the wrong decision, fear of failure or making a mistake, fear of ... The list is endless. But the fact is, change is and always will be inevitable – except, as some humorist once put it, from a vending machine! Change has to happen otherwise there would be no progress. Everyone knows this and accepts it as fact but, on the whole, nobody likes change. As Mark Twain once wrote:

"The only person who likes change is a wet baby."

My advice to you, here, is simply this: accept that change is necessary and that it's going to happen, with or without you. You may have your doubts and concerns, you may be frightened or worried, but, as I've said, the only way to overcome those feelings is to jump into action and work them to death! In other words, don't let fear get hold of you. Don't be like the caterpillar who looked up and saw a butterfly, then turned to his brother and said, "Huh, there's no way you'd get me up there in one of those things!" Accept that change has to happen; plan and prepare for it properly and then go along with it wholeheartedly. Of course, sometimes the change might not be for the best, but that doesn't necessarily mean that the change was wrong, it just means that you have to persevere and change again until you find a better solution. It's like fishing: if your bait isn't working you don't stick with it, and you don't pack up your rod and go home. Instead, you change the bait and you keep changing it until you find one that works.

So, then, accept that change has to happen, plan and prepare for it properly, and then go along with it wholeheartedly, and also, try not to worry. Yes, I know that's easier said than done but you'd do well to remember these words from author, Corrie Ten Boom:

"Worry does not empty tomorrow of its sorrow;
it only saps today of its strength."

I trust you will not allow that to happen.

Until next time, then, I remain once again,

Yours cordially,
Uncle Bob

Chapter Six
A Word of Wisdom

Don't let your learning lead to knowledge. Let it lead to action.
Jim Rohn (speaker, trainer and writer)

Dear _ _ _ _ _ _ _ (fill in your name),

Someone once said, "Experience is the hardest kind of teaching, because it gives you the test first and the lesson afterwards." The Irish poet and dramatist, Oscar Wilde, said much the same thing, when he wrote:

"Experience is the name that everyone gives to their mistakes."

If there is one lesson that I, personally, wish I could have learnt earlier in life, it would be to listen; to listen and not feel the need to talk all the time. Now that may seem like quite an admission from someone who does a considerable amount of public speaking but, if the truth be told, the ability to listen is a far greater gift than the ability to speak, at least in my opinion.

Some people are surprised to learn that, privately, I am somewhat of an introvert and can often be quite reserved. A far cry from the popular image of the powerful, dynamic speaker with the outgoing personality! The truth is, I have always made a good living from using one of the smallest muscles in the human body – the tongue – and I very much enjoy doing so, but it also has to be said that using that piece of my anatomy has also caused me more than a bit of trouble in my time! Indeed, sometimes we would all do a lot better to 'zip the lip,' as it were. In fact, the older I get the more I come to appreciate the well-known-but-not-so-well-practised, 'two ears and one mouth' rule. We *really* should listen twice as much as we speak. Besides which, holding our tongue and listening is also acknowledged to be complimentary to the speaker; as the saying goes: A good listener is a silent flatterer.

This letter, then, is dedicated to the topic of listening and learning – which is the secret to all knowledge, as you are about to find out in the following story.

Legend has it that an ambitious youth once approached an old sage seeking to learn the wisdom of enlightenment. "O wise and knowledgeable master," said the youth, "How can I discover the wisdom of the ages?" The sage looked at the youth thoughtfully and then replied with the words of an ancient proverb (you might have to read this next bit slowly):

> He who knows not, and knows not that he
> knows not – is a fool, shun him;
> He who knows not, and knows that he knows
> not – is a child, teach him.
> He who knows, and knows not that he
> knows – is asleep, wake him.
> He who knows, and knows that he knows – is
> wise, follow him.

The youth nodded and replied reverently, "O wise and knowledgeable master, I know that I do not know, but I am keen and willing to follow." "Then," said the sage, "Follow quietly, and listen very carefully, and I will reveal to you the secret of all knowledge." The youth followed him eagerly, but the sage became silent and said nothing more. After five minutes, or so, of absolute silence the youth finally said, "I'm listening, O knowledgeable master." The wise old sage turned slowly to look at him, smiled and then replied: "Now you are learning!"

In a training seminar, if I ask a number of people how they think they can improve on their management, sales or communication skills, most will say something along the lines of; be more commanding, decisive, persuasive, confident, or to sharpen their selling skills, or their public speaking skills, etc. Few, if any, will mention a desire to become a better listener! (People don't like to admit that they are poor listeners.) When it comes to communicating, most people tend to place too much importance on the qualities to do with speech and too little on listening. And yet, in itself, listening is the single most flattering, disarming, persuasive and powerful technique there is in effective communication. Listening shows people that you care enough to actually hear what they have to say. Listening attentively also enables you to learn what you might otherwise miss. (Incidentally, have you noticed how the word 'learn' incorporates the words 'ear' and 'earn'?)

Ralph Waldo Emerson was a learned man known to have an attentive ear for others. He once said, "Every man I meet is in some way superior and I can learn from him." Truly, listening is the key to all knowledge.

Recently, I helped out and accompanied my young son, and the rest of his classmates, on a field trip to learn more about the countryside. Prior to our setting out the children were all gathered around in excited and noisy anticipation. Eventually, the teacher called for quiet and then proceeded to issue a few warnings and last-minute instructions. One of those instructions was that the children should remember to be quiet and to listen out for the various wildlife. "After all, children," said the teacher, "What happens if your mouth is open all the time?" In answer to the question all the children replied in unison, "Your brains fly out!" I smiled, but that statement is not far from the truth. If your mouth is open all the time because you are continuously talking, then your brains – or lack of them – really do fly out. Remember that one of the reasons the owl is considered wise is because it keeps its mouth shut most of the time! This little rhyme by Edward H. Richards reiterates the point:

> A wise old owl sat on an oak,
> The more he saw the less he spoke,
> The less he spoke the more he heard,
> Why aren't we like that wise old bird?

The reason, unfortunately, is that we, as human beings, tend to care more about what *we* have to say about our own wants and needs and desires, than we do about other people's. It is not merely a coincidence that the most widely used word in the English language is 'I', followed closely by 'me', 'myself' and 'my'. In this competitive, dog-eat-dog world of ours it seems to be more a case of everyone for themselves! Dorothy Leeds puts it like this:

> "Everyone has a secret radio station called 'WII FM' – otherwise known as, 'What's In It For Me?'"

Now, of course, that is a rather cynical picture and although it may seem close to the truth sometimes, it is not really accurate. You see, it doesn't have to be like that and, indeed, very often it's not. The fact is, there are more than a few individuals who still believe in the philosophy of putting others first. These tend to be the same individuals who have more than just a few friends, real friends. They are the ones who stand out from the crowd, the ones who find real meaning in life and who discover that true success and happiness is found in serving, in frequently putting the interests of others before themselves, in taking the time and being bothered enough to care.

Dale Carnegie, in his book, *How to Win Friends and Influence People*, wrote:

> "You can make more friends in two months by becoming interested in other people than you can in two years trying to get other people interested in you."

On a similar but more humorous note, Dr William King observed:

> "A gossip is one who talks to you about other people; a bore is one who talks to you about himself, and a brilliant conversationalist is one who talks to you about yourself."

Someone else once quipped: "It's all right to hold a conversation as long as you let go of it once in a while." What are these experts saying? Simply this: if you want to make friends, if you want to make a good impression – if you want to learn – ask the right questions and then listen, attentively, for all you are worth. And what are the right questions? I'll let Rudyard Kipling answer that with the lines from his verse, 'Six Honest Serving Men,' taken from *The Elephant's Child.*

Six Honest Serving Men

I keep six honest serving men,
(They taught me all I knew);
Their names are What and Why and When
and How and Where and Who.

Rudyard Kipling

In short, you need to ask what, why, when, how, where and who questions. What better way of inviting conversation, what better way of communicating, and what better way of listening and learning and making a good impression? Here are a few examples to give you a feel for what I'm getting at:

♦ **WHAT**: What can I do for you? What seems to be the problem? What can I get for you? What is it that you're not telling me? What's the matter? What would you like to see happen?

♦ **WHY**: Why is it so important to you? Why don't you tell me about it? Why do you feel that way? Why don't you let me do that for you? Why are you worried? Why not try this and see if it helps?

♦ **WHEN**: When would you like to talk? When can we get together? When did you say it was going to happen? Whenever you want me just call, okay?

♦ **HOW**: How are you really? How are things at home? How are you getting on at work? How are you going to manage to do that? How can I help you? How about us getting together?

♦ **WHERE**: Where can I meet you? Where does it hurt? Where do your preferences lie? Where do you want to start? Where can I help?

♦ **WHO**: Who cares what other people think? Who can really stop you if you put your mind to it? Who is it that you need to speak to? Who can help? Who could do that for you?

Listening requires more than just hearing, it requires concentration as well. I've read that a little while ago, on the radio, the UK Minister of Education, the Rt Hon. David Blunkett, was being interviewed. During the interview, the question was put to Mr Blunkett as to whether or not he considered his blindness to be a disadvantage in the House of Commons or in carrying out his duties as a minister. He replied that rather than being a drawback, he considered his disability was, in actual fact, an advantage to some degree. His reasoning was that, in only being able to listen to what people had to say, he had to really listen to them! Remember, listening requires more than just hearing, it also requires your concentration.

Prior to writing this letter, I researched my archives of reference and training materials for any relevant information. Here's an anagram I came across that offers some good advice for becoming a better listener. Unfortunately, the original author remains anonymous to me but, whoever it was, they understood that the first rung on the ladder to success is to listen.

L: Look into the eyes of the person speaking to you.
A: Ask questions.
D: Don't interrupt.
D: Don't change the subject.
E: Empathise.
R: Respond both verbally and non-verbally.

This 'ladder' is, indeed, good advice for learning how to listen more attentively. I especially recommend the first step, looking into the eyes of the person speaking to you. Maintaining eye contact shows sincerity and warmth. It shows the speaker that you are, in fact, listening and so encourages him to continue or elaborate. Maintaining eye contact also helps you to focus on the conversation and so not get distracted by other things.

Let me move on, now, and show you how to listen and effectively deal with a customer complaint; in fact, any complaint. The way *not* to do it, is to give as good as you get: use some fine-sounding argument to try and get the customer to see sense or to beat him or her into submission. If you do that you might win the battle but, ultimately, you'll lose the war. As the 18th century English poet, William Blake, pointed out:

"A mind convinced against its will is of the same opinion still."

No! The way to effectively deal with a customer complaint is simply this: pay attention and listen to what *they* have to say. Don't argue or dispute with them, don't acknowledge or return insults or accusations or excuses, just bite your tongue – until it bleeds if you have to!

In other words, let the customer (or, to broaden the situation, your employee or spouse or whoever) have his or her say without you interrupting or jumping straight in on the defensive. A dissatisfied customer can very easily become an irate customer, ranting and raving and fuming because of ill-treatment or poor service or faulty goods, etc. But it doesn't have to be this way. You see, a complaining customer is like an over-stretched balloon, tense and filled with hot air to the point of bursting! Now, if salespeople jump straight on to the defensive or even into a counterattack – if they retaliate, if they are rude or apathetic about the customer's concerns – this is like taking a pin to the balloon. The balloon explodes!

However, salespeople could simply pay attention to what the customer has to say, listen with empathy and resist the temptation to speak – regardless of how unjust the accusations might be. This is like holding the neck of the balloon and slowly allowing the hot air to be released until, eventually, the balloon is completely deflated, so the aggression is spent. Irate customers are often so relieved at having been able vent their frustration, they become more amiable, or even apologetic for having bent your ear so much.

At the end of the day, our reaction to a verbal attack, in whatever area, comes down to a matter of choice. As the author, Bob Gass, puts it:

> "Pride says, 'Don't just stand there, say something!' Wisdom says, 'Don't just say something, stand there!'"

In other words, sometimes the wisest thing to do is let the moment pass before you open your mouth. My grandmother used to say it like this: "Count to ten and think before you speak." The Bible tells us:

> "A man of knowledge uses words with restraint, and a man of understanding is even-tempered. Even a fool is thought wise if he keeps silent, and discerning if he holds his tongue."
> (Proverbs 17:27–28)

Listen, now, to some further words of wisdom in the form of this verse, written by James S. Hewitt.

"The boneless tongue, so small and weak,
Can crush and kill," declares the Greek,
"The tongue destroys a greater horde,"
The Turk asserts, "than does the sword."

The Persian proverb wisely saith,
"A lengthy tongue – an early death!"
Or sometimes takes this form instead,
"Do not let your tongue cut off your head."

"The tongue can speak a word whose speed,"
Say the Chinese, "outstrips the steed."
The Arab sages said in part,
"The tongue's great storehouse is the heart."

From Hebrew was the maxim sprung,
"Thy feet should slip, but ne'er the tongue."
The sacred writer crowns the whole,
"Who keeps the tongue doth keep his soul."

James S. Hewitt

Following on from this verse let me now offer a word or two about criticism. Sometimes we have a responsibility to criticise others. We should not shy away from doing this if it is necessary. But probably the best piece of advice that I have ever received on this subject is this: If it will be painful for you to criticise someone then you are probably safe to do it, but if you will take any pleasure from it, hold your tongue! In other words, ask yourself whether this is constructive criticism or destructive criticism, and be honest with your answer. Let me put it another way; before you criticise, reprimand or offer your opinion, **THINK**: is it **T**ruthful, is it **H**elpful, is it **I**mportant, is it **N**eeded, is it **K**indly? Then let your conscience, your inner voice, determine what action you should take.

Well, in this letter I set out to address the subject of learning through listening but the message wouldn't be complete without some mention of learning through study or reading. Lastly, then, I want to strongly recommend that you do just that. Study, read and learn everything you can so that you will always be an expert at what you do or whatever it is that interests you.

Charlie ('Tremendous') Jones, in his book, *Life is Tremendous*, puts it like this:

> "You will be the same in five years time as you are today, except for the people you meet and the books you read."

I firmly agree with that statement, and so I very much want to encourage you to become an avid reader if you're not already. Now, obviously, I know that you are reading this book – and I'm happy about that – but what I'm talking about here is not just reading one, or even two, books, but reading every book you can lay your hands on. Every book that interests you, that is, but especially books that will help and teach you as, indeed, I hope this one will do. Granted, this will cost you in both time and money but, as Benjamin Franklin once said:

> "If you empty the pennies from your pocket into your mind, your mind will fill your pockets with pennies."

However, if you get yourself a library card you won't even have to spend any money, because libraries provide knowledge for free – all you have to do is take your own container! (On the point of spending money, it never ceases to amaze me how some people think nothing of splashing out $50 or $60 a head on a meal – food for the stomach – but yet, those very same people become penny-pinchers when it comes to investing in a good book or audio programme – food for the mind. They don't seem to realise that the nourishment from the meal lasts for only 24 hours whereas the benefits of investing in personal development last for a lifetime!)

So then, let me encourage you, once again, to become an avid reader. Read everything you can on your chosen subject and become an expert at what you do or whatever it is that interests you. Remember this, leaders are readers. Remember, also, that reading keeps you growing! And that's worth investing in – don't you think?

Yours cordially,
Uncle Bob

Chapter Seven

Contending with Non-Success

When you fail, you have two choices: get better or get bitter.
Les Brown (author and motivational speaker)

Dear _ _ _ _ _ _ _ (fill in your name),

Do you like fruitcake? I do! I love a mug of tea and a large chunk of rich, moist, fruitcake! In fact, that's exactly what I've just consumed as I contemplated sitting down to write this letter. Now, before you start thinking that I might have become a bit of a 'fruitcake' in sharing this, let me also share a parallel with you.

To fully appreciate a good fruitcake you need to devour it slowly and, of course, one piece at a time. If you tried to eat the whole cake in one sitting it would probably make you sick. Why? Because the whole cake is far too rich to eat in one go. There is simply too much of it to be able to digest it all at once. This is also the case with these letters, which are the accumulation of over 30 years of knowledge gleaned from my own personal experiences, as well as from many other different sources far too numerous to mention here. For you to be able to take everything in and devour the 'lore' in just one sitting would be impossible. You just can't cram decades of amassed knowledge and experience into a few hours of reading and expect to be able to learn and retain everything. And even if you could, the information would be far too rich; too difficult to fully appreciate.

A good fruitcake will last for months, even years, and the longer you take to eat it the better it will taste because it matures and develops as time goes by. Likewise with these letters: to get the most out of them you need to revisit them every once in a while. It's fine to start at page one and read right the way through: doing so will, I hope, whet your appetite, encourage you and inspire you to greater heights. However, you need to understand that inspiration is always short-lived. No one stays on a high 24 hours a day, 7 days a week, 52 weeks a year. The fact is, there are going to be difficult times ahead. Life is not sunshine and flowers all the time; you have to go through your dark winter days as well. US entertainer Dolly Parton once put it like this:

> "If you want the rainbow you have to be willing to put up with the rain."

That's true. If you want to win and succeed in life you have to put up with some dull rainy days and even a few storms, but this is where your character is built and refined. (I shall be writing about character-building later, in Chapter 12.) Indeed, life is most definitely not plain-sailing; rather it's a mixed bag of peaks and troughs, of ups and downs. What I am going to suggest, therefore, is that you re-read these letters, especially during your winter periods, your troughs or lows, as it were.

This advice is especially pertinent to the subject I am going to be writing to you about now, namely, non-success. (I call it, 'non-success' because the closest alternative – 'failure' – seems such a definite and final-sounding word, and non-success should never be final.) You see, anyone can read about contending with non-success when they are succeeding and enjoying life, but the time when you really need to read this letter again, (and the other letters too) is when you are in the midst of one of those winter periods and you are seeking to find the sunshine again!

Let me begin this subject, then, by stating that the only major difference between a successful person and a failure is simply this: the successful person kept on trying.

Sir Edmund Hillary is living proof of this. You may remember that he and his Nepalese guide were the very first men to, literally, stand on top of the world. It was 11.30 in the morning, on 29 May 1953, when Edmund Hillary and the Nepalese Sherpa, Tenzing Norgay, finally placed the British flag on top of Mount Everest, which at 8,848 metres above sea level is the highest point on earth.

Hillary had been on Mount Everest in 1951 and again in 1952, both times in a serious attempt to reach the summit. Unfortunately, both attempts were unsuccessful, but his exploits did bring him to the attention of the Royal Geographic Society and the Alpine Club of Great Britain. After they had agreed to sponsor him for a third attempt in 1953, Hillary made an emotional address to their members. It's reported that he was welcomed on to the stage by thunderous applause as the audience recognised his previous efforts. Hillary was overcome; he moved away from the microphone and turned towards a picture of Everest. Then he made a defiant fist and as he pointed to the mountain he said in a loud voice, "You beat me once, you beat me twice, but, Mount Everest, you will not beat me again, because you have grown all you are going to, but I am still growing!" Edmund Hillary succeeded on that third attempt. He was a failure who kept on trying and, indeed, one who continues to do so today. Now, at age 80, Sir Edmund Hillary (he was knighted for his achievement) is no longer mountain-climbing. Instead, today he devotes his energies to environmental issues and the needs of the Nepalese people.

There are plenty more examples, in the pages of our history books and even our daily newspapers, of this success-achieved-through-failure process, and, indeed, we shall look at more examples later. But, for now, I want to make it clear that success and failure work together, hand in glove. You simply can't achieve one without experiencing the other, not in the long run anyway. There's an old saying that puts it well:

> Success is the result of good judgement; good judgement the result of experience, and experience the result of bad judgement.

Face it, non-success happens, but non-success doesn't mean that you are a failure; it just means that you have to try again; it means, not this time but maybe the next, or the next. The question is, how much do you want success? (Enough to start over?)

Non-success means you have a fresh opportunity to do just that, start over again, but this time you'll have the benefit of hindsight on your side. Certainly, failing is demotivating, demoralising, depressing, discouraging, disheartening and every other negative word beginning with the letter 'd' but, hey! no one ever said success was easy. In fact, it most definitely is not, which is why the rewards are so great for those few who achieve it. As Vince Lombardi used to say:

> "It's not whether you get knocked down, it's whether you get up that counts."

The key to success is to keep getting up or, at least, to get up one more time than you fall down. The American TV celebrity and motivational speaker, Les Brown (also husband of Gladys Knight) says:

> "When life knocks you down, try to fall on your back because if you can look up you can get up."

In other words, if you set your sights high, and remain focused on your objective, if you keep looking upwards and see what needs to be done, then you won't lose sight of your vision and you won't be tempted to give up; well at least not so easily!

Unfortunately, many people don't heed this advice. They fall at the first hurdle and their defeat so deflates them that they give up and never try again – too many painful memories! If only these people would realise that their previous failures are just evidence that at least they tried to do something. If only they would understand that the greatest mistake of all is to be afraid of making another one. If they would only let go of their mistakes and try again, then they would see that success could very well be waiting for them right around the next corner.

We all make mistakes, every last one of us – as they say, 'Nobody's perfect.' Understand, then, that looking backwards with remorse or regret is not the way forwards. You can't move ahead when you're in reverse! It's okay to look back and learn from your past – that's a good thing – but then you must let go of the past and look forward again. It's like using the rear-view mirror in your car: when you are driving you are meant to glance into it fleetingly not stare into it constantly! So then, let go of your mistakes, get into gear, look ahead and move forwards again.

Let me illustrate further with this example. In some parts of India the locals have a technique for catching monkeys, which they then sell in the marketplace. The technique is very simple and works like this: first of all, they put some tempting titbits of food, maybe some fruit and nuts, into a heavy glass bottle which has a narrow mouth. They then secure the bottle to the ground or to the base of a tree, sprinkle a few more titbits around it, and leave it alone for a while. The monkey comes along, puts his hand through the narrow mouth of the bottle and grabs a fistful of goodies. This is the monkey's mistake! You see, the monkey can't get its clenched fist back out of the bottle, and it doesn't have the sense to simply let go of its treasure! It becomes trapped in a blunder of its own making. Let me say it one more time, let go of your mistakes and move on. Don't allow non-success to become permanent failure; don't allow non-success to imprison you.

Here's a piece of prose that has been around for a while and one that communicates the real meaning of failure. May I suggest this as good reading for those hard times, when you need to remind yourself to let go and move on?

> Failure does not mean I am a failure;
> It does mean I have not yet succeeded.
> Failure does not mean I have accomplished nothing;
> It does mean I have learned something.
> Failure does not mean I have been a fool;
> It does mean I had enough faith to experiment.
> Failure does not mean I have been disgraced;
> It does mean I dared to try.
> Failure does not mean I don't have it in me;
> It does mean that I might have to do it differently.
> Failure does not mean I am inferior;
> It does mean I am not perfect.
> Failure does not mean I have wasted my time;
> It does mean I have an excuse to start again.
> Failure does not mean I should give up;
> It does mean I must try harder.
> Failure does not mean I will never make it;
> It does mean I need more patience.
> *Anonymous*

Remember, a successful person is just a failure who kept on trying. Here are some more examples of people, including myself, who did just that.

Back in the mid-1990s a business venture that I was heavily involved in was declared bankrupt, due to the unfortunate financial collapse of my close friend and, at that time, business partner. Being a partnership and not a limited company I stood to lose an awful lot of money if the company went into receivership. Needless to say, I fought tooth and nail against this happening and eventually, by means far too lengthy to explain here, I managed to beg, borrow and steal (steal only from myself, of course!) my way to having my business partner's bankruptcy overturned. Those were very dark days for me and there was a threat – albeit hard to say how real – of my losing everything, including our home! In the face of this 'non-success', I gained the strength that I needed to persevere by praying and by reading, often, this verse from the Bible:

> "Commit your way to the LORD; trust in him and he will do this: He will make your righteousness shine like the dawn, the justice of your cause like the noonday sun." (Psalm 37: 5–6)

Eventually, after much struggle and turmoil things did work out. In fact, in the end they worked out very well indeed. Some two and a half years later the business was sold for a considerable sum. I give the credit for all of this to God who, as the Bible tells us, is an ever-present help in times of trouble. But I'd like to suggest that you discover this for yourself.

For a more shining example, no doubt you will have heard the name 'Birdseye,' synonymous with the frozen food industry. Clarence E. Birdseye (1886–1956) was successful, in that he was another failure who simply kept on trying. In 1924 he lost all that he had on his failed frozen food enterprise, including money borrowed against a life-insurance policy! But 'Captain Birdseye,' as the television ads portray him, didn't give up. Instead, with just US $7 in cash and the loan of some space in a friend's ice factory, he started out again and began experimenting in methods for freezing and preserving foods for later use.

Some five years later, he sold his frozen food company for US $22 million, so that he could concentrate on experimenting and coming up with new inventions. He went on to register nearly 300 patents in all. Clarence Birdseye was a man of character, a man who understood that failure is an event and not a person.

The Scottish historian and essayist, Thomas Carlyle (1795–1881), became a wealthy and very successful writer after the publication of his three volumes on *The French Revolution*. However, Carlyle was another who experienced more than a little non-success.

It was through his friend in London, John Stuart Mill (the famous philosopher and economist), that Carlyle first became interested in the French Revolution. In time, that interest led Carlyle to start writing what would eventually become a masterpiece of modern-day literature. However, it wasn't all plain sailing! After five months of continuous writing, Carlyle finished the first volume, which he then passed over to his friend, John Mill, so that he could give it his professional opinion. Unfortunately, whilst the manuscript was in Mill's care, a maid lighting a fire accidentally burnt it. The whole thing, all of five months' work, up in smoke! Mill was devastated and horrified at the loss as, indeed, anyone would be, but Carlyle never uttered a single word of condemnation. Of course, he was upset – who wouldn't be? But instead of dwelling on the defeat, the *non-success*, Carlyle sat down and started out again from scratch!

I recently experienced a similar situation myself, when I was working on a manuscript for an audio programme (published by Simon & Schuster Audio). Fortunately, I only lost a few weeks worth of work, not five months worth! Nonetheless, I know how absolutely drained and demoralised I felt when my computer crashed without my having created any back-up disks! There was nothing else for it but to follow Carlyle's example and start again. It was a laborious struggle for me, but I can't even begin to comprehend the lengths he must have gone to. Thomas Carlyle was, indeed, a success; he was someone who tasted defeat, but it wasn't to his liking so he spat it out and kept on trying!

Another similar example can be found in the story of Thomas Edison and the destruction of his laboratory in New Jersey, USA. This laboratory was Edison's pride and joy; he affectionately called it his 'invention factory'. In 1914, however, the whole plant was burned to the ground. There was more than $2 million worth of damage, but the buildings were only insured for about 12 per cent of that amount. To make matters worse, much of Edison's life's work also went up in the flames.

Edison, himself, watched the disaster with remarkable composure. In fact, during the height of the blaze his son, Charles Edison, reported that he came across his father calmly watching the scene. "Where's your mother?" his father asked him. "Quickly, go and find her and bring her here, for she will never see anything quite like this as long as she lives." (What an attitude.) The following day Edison began scribbling down his ideas for starting again. He was 67 years of age. "Thank God, all of our mistakes have been destroyed," he said. "In a new factory we can start our experiments with a clean slate." And of course, he went on to do just that!

As a final example, no one today would doubt that Abraham Lincoln was a successful man. In fact, Lincoln's name has gone down in the history books as one of the greatest American presidents of all time. Nevertheless, the life of Abraham Lincoln has got to be one of the best examples of the success-achieved-through-failure process that I have ever come across. Lincoln was a man who just would not quit. He was a man who epitomises the rule that a success is just a failure who kept on trying. Here's a brief outline of his life:

- In 1816, at the age of 7, his family were compelled to move out of their home, and he had to go to work with his father to help support them.

- In 1818, at the age of 9, his mother died.

- In 1831 he left home, started a business and subsequently failed in it!

- In 1832 he moved into politics and ran for the post of Illinois State Legislator. He was defeated at the ballot box!

- Also in 1832 he lost his job and only source of income when the store where he worked closed down. In the same year he also failed to gain acceptance into law school.

- In 1833 he borrowed money, and with a friend (as a partner), bought a store and started a new business. A few months later the friend died. The business failed and Lincoln was left with debts of over $1,000, which took him the next 17 years to pay off.

- In 1834 he ran for the Illinois State Legislator post again. This time he won!

- In 1835 the girl that he hoped to marry, Ann Rutledge, suddenly died of 'brain fever'. She was just 19 and Lincoln was heartbroken.

- In 1836 he suffered a nervous breakdown and was in bed for six months.

- In 1837 he proposed marriage to an old friend, Mary Owens, but she refused him.

- In 1838 he attempted to become speaker of the State Legislator, but was defeated.

- In 1840 he attempted to become Municipal Legislator but, again, he was defeated.

- In 1843 he stood for Congress. He lost again.

- In 1846 he stood for Congress again. This time he won!

- In 1848 he stood for re-election to Congress and lost his seat.

- In 1849 he returned home to Springfield and applied for the post of Commissioner for the General Land Office. Again he was unsuccessful.

- In 1854 he stood for election to the United States Senate. He lost.

- In 1856 he sought to be nominated as the Vice President at the Republican party's national convention. He lost, having only received 110 votes!

- In 1858 he stood for the US Senate again, and again he lost.

- But then in 1860 Abraham Lincoln won the biggest election of them all, when the people of the United States voted him into office as President.

The one thing that all the above examples share – in fact, the common trait in all successful men and women – is persistence in the face of adversity, coupled with a firm resolve to accomplish a worthwhile goal. It's not as though the winners in life are unaffected by defeat or that they are immune to feeling drained and devoid of the will to continue. Every human being is susceptible to such feelings. Rather, it is because the winner's resolve to continue in some worthwhile endeavour is stronger (although not always by much), than their will to call it a day and give up.

Of course, the attribute of endurance plays a major role, as we saw earlier (in Chapter 1), but the real key here is found in the word 'goal'. The winners in life are always passionate about something, they have a real deep-down interest or desire or goal, and it's the goal, in itself, that drives them forward. Leonardo da Vinci understood this. He wrote:

> "Obstacles cannot crush me; every obstacle yields to firm resolve."

Let me reiterate, then, that success and non-success work together hand in glove. You simply can't achieve one without experiencing the other. The fact is, you are going to lose, at least some of the time. That is an absolute certainty! But here's another fact: you can turn those losses into advantages, you can learn from them, you can grow from them and you can turn them around and capitalise on them. So, you could say that non-success is actually good for you! Here are ten different reasons why:

1. It makes you appreciate success when it does happen.

2. It develops endurance and stamina.

3. It provides you with a learning experience.

4. It keeps you humble.

5. It can, sometimes, be a blessing in disguise.

6. It allows you to empathise with, and help, others in similar situations.

7. It protects you if you're not yet ready to handle success.

8. It shows you who your real friends are!

9. It builds character and motivates you to try again.

10. It means you're more likely to sustain success when it does arrive.

Let's now take a closer look at some of these reasons and see why non-success is both necessary and good for you at times. Well, the first thing about non-success is that it keeps you humble. Someone once said:

> "If you could kick the person most responsible for your troubles, you wouldn't be able to sit down for a week!"

When you realise and accept that non-success is no one else's fault but your own, it humbles you, and as the saying goes, with humility comes wisdom!

Sometimes, non-success also protects us. (Think how grateful you should be that some people fail their driving tests!) Sometimes it can even be a blessing in disguise. How many times have you looked back, with hindsight, and realised that your non-success actually turned out to be the best thing for you. It just might very well be that you were meant to fail! At least now you are free to take advantage of that new opportunity that's waiting around the next corner! After all, remember what they say: for every door that closes another one opens!

Experiencing defeat, though, always makes your success taste that much sweeter when you do finally achieve it. Failing makes you appreciate winning. Think about it. If success were handed to you on a plate, it wouldn't take long before contempt for it set in. That's the reason why so many rich kids get a bad reputation. If a child is spoilt – if their every desire and whim is given in to – if the trappings of success are handed to them on a plate, they become contemptuous of it; they take everything for granted and have no respect or appreciation for hard work. On the other hand, when you have to overcome obstacles and setbacks, when you have to work long hard hours in order to achieve success, then you learn to appreciate success when it happens.

Similarly, it is only through weathering the storms of life that we mature and develop strength and character. Consider, for a moment, what happens to a young tree or sapling. If the tree is over-watered by frequent rains, then it will not send its roots deep down into the earth searching for moisture. Instead, the root system remains near the surface and the plant flourishes, but only during the time of plenty. However, come the first spell of dry weather, the tree is prone to wither and die because it has not had to develop any real foundations to sustain it. Non-success, then, helps you to develop endurance and character. Again, take nature as an example: what happens if you break a spider's web, or disturb a bird's nest, or knock over an ant hill, or pilfer some honey from a beehive, or take the wool off a sheep's back or draw a pail of milk from a cow? I'll tell you what happens, they simply start afresh and begin production all over again. So then, take a lesson from

Mother Nature and whenever a setback occurs, just grit your teeth and start over.

Non-success also gives you the opportunity to learn from your mistakes and consider how to do it better next time. This anonymous poem about sums it up:

> For every problem under the sun,
> There's a solution or there's none.
> If there's a solution, then go and find it.
> And if there isn't, then never mind it.

In other words, don't mope around feeling sorry for yourself, don't let your setback become like a brick wall that you can't see over or around. Instead, stand back, take a fresh look and see the problem for what it really is: an obstacle, not an impenetrable obstruction. If you take a small pebble and hold it up close to your eye it will fill your whole vision. But move your head backwards and you see the object for what it really is: something inconsequential and tiny in comparison to the whole picture. So then, stand back, look at your defeat or problem in the cool, clear light of day, then seek to find a way around it and move on.

Well, it's about time for me to wrap things up and move on! Before I do, though, let me relate one last story to remind you, again, not to let your non-success become permanent failure. In fact, a good title for this story would be, "Don't let your non-success bury you".

Not so long ago, a mule, belonging to a local farmer, fell into an old disused well. The mule brayed incessantly and stomped about in the confined space but it was no good; it was stuck. The distraught animal was just too far down and the farmer, try as he might, couldn't pull him out. It was hopeless! Finally, the saddened farmer resigned himself to putting the mule out of its misery. As he didn't have a gun, he decided that the best thing for it would be to fill the well with earth and bury the hapless animal. The old man fetched his truck and swallowed hard as he tipped the first load of earth into the well. The mule panicked and instead of letting itself be buried, it kicked and stomped even more. In fact, the mule stomped so much that it trampled the earth down under its hooves and ended up climbing on top of it. The same thing happened with the second and the third load. Each time, the mule would stomp and kick and trample the earth down, and each time the mule got higher and higher up the well shaft. Finally, the mule made it to the top and jumped free, having learnt a very valuable lesson.

Let me say it one more time: don't allow your non-success to bury you alive; don't allow it to become a permanent failure! Remember, successful people are just failures that kept on trying – so, keep on keeping on! And until next time I remain, once again,

Yours cordially,
Uncle Bob

Chapter Eight
Finding Inspiration

*The biggest mistake a person can make is to
believe they are working for someone else.*
Anonymous

Dear _ _ _ _ _ _ _ (fill in your name),

I'm often asked what it is that motivates me, what switches me on
and where I find my inspiration. I wish there were an easy answer
to that question, but the fact is, I get inspired by lots of things. I
can say, however, that overall – in my work as a writer, speaker
and trainer – my inspiration comes from my desire to encourage
and inspire others and from my aspirations to pass on what I have
learnt myself. You could say, I aspire to inspire before, and after,
I expire! This is what I see as my calling or purpose in life; and it's
this calling that inspires me to do what I do. Besides that, I love
what I do so much so that it would be more accurate to call it a
hobby or a favourite pursuit than it would be to call it work!
Confucius said it best when he wrote:

> "Choose a job you love, and you will never have to work a day in
> your life."

What better way of finding inspiration than doing what you love
and loving what you do? So, the long and the short of it comes
down to this: to find inspiration, first know what your purpose is
and then always be working towards it.

Now, of course, that's all very well and fine-sounding, but what
about finding the inspiration for the daily, run-of-the-mill, mundane
things that still have to be done? What about finding inspiration

when you don't feel motivated? How can you switch yourself – or others – on when you don't feel like being switched on? That question is not so easy to answer. The thing is, everyone must find his or her own inspiration and there is nothing that you or I, nor anyone else for that matter, can do to motivate someone who doesn't want to be motivated. Finding inspiration, then, is down to each individual. Nobody can find it for you and there is no magic formula. After saying that, however, I hope in this letter to at least give you a few pointers in the right direction.

To start with, I assume that you purchased this book (or someone else purchased it for you), because you are self-motivated. But what was it that initially motivated you to pick up this book and start reading it? It may be that the title intrigued you first, but after that it most likely was your desire for personal development, for success and achievement, that caused you to buy or 'buy into' this book. That being the case, you already know, in part at least, the answer to finding inspiration. You have to do something, you have to move into action, you have to stop yakking and get cracking! Sometimes you just have to begin whatever it is and then inspiration catches you up, much the same as it does when you start to read a good book.

Appreciate, however, that others will have picked this book up too, but, unlike yourself, they put it straight back down again. These people are also seeking success, they too are seeking inspiration and the answers to some of life's questions, but they ended up putting the book back on the shelf again because they weren't and aren't motivated enough to actually do anything about it. Instead, they are looking for an easy option; they are looking for someone else to do it for them. Even if a book, such as this one, were to be given to them for free, they probably wouldn't read it because they can't be bothered. And as I've said, you can't motivate somebody who doesn't want to be motivated.

This reminds me of a recent speech I gave for a Footsie 100 company. (That is, one of *The Financial Times* Stock Exchange's top 100 companies.) Several hundred delegates were gathered together for an annual sales conference in a top hotel in Brighton, England. I was invited to speak at the close of the conference and I must have done a reasonable job because a few days later I received a glowing testimonial letter from the Vice President of the company, who had been in attendance! Of course, I was very pleased to receive the commendation, but on the day itself, I had been a little disappointed. You see, I knew that I had not been able to reach everybody and that there were some people in the audience who simply weren't switched on! Certainly, there were more than a few who were. You can generally spot them a mile off, especially the ones who rapidly bounce their knees up and down because their enthusiasm won't allow them to sit still. However, there were a few individuals who seemed to be completely disinterested, as if it were hard for them to stay awake! I have always found this situation frustrating, and no doubt always will, but again, you just can't reach or motivate somebody who doesn't want to be reached or motivated.

In fact, all the motivational tools in the world – be they books, tapes, seminars, speakers, bonuses, incentives or whatever – will always be completely ineffectual unless a person actually wants to be affected by them. It is only when you want to change your life for the better that you will be open to, and indeed find, the motivation needed to do so.

Going back to our question, then, how can you find inspiration for the daily, run-of-the-mill, mundane things that have to be done? How can you switch yourself on? Well, here are the two things that work best for me. (Note: there are a dozen different ways to help motivate yourself listed in Chapter 6 of my previous book *Maximise Your Potential*.)

1. Goal-setting

Now, I don't mean mapping out your entire life or planning ahead for the next however long. (We have already covered this in Chapter 3.) Remember I am talking here about finding *daily* inspiration, so when I say goal-setting I'm talking here more about a daily planner or a 'things-to-do' list.

You know, I'd go as far as to say that my daily 'things-to-do' list is where I find most of my motivation. My list is my plan, my blueprint for the day, my inspiration to accomplish that which I set out to do. Without it my sense of daily purpose is diminished. That's not to say that I wouldn't have a productive day without it. Rather, my sense of accomplishment is not as great if I don't get to see my achievements in black and white; if I don't get the pleasure of striking through an item and marking it off my list as 'DONE'. Sometimes my 'things-to-do' list drives me up the wall. Sometimes it becomes almost an obsession to tick everything off as having been accomplished. Sometimes, especially if I'm frustrated, I even consider striking an item off my list (without actually having completed the task) just for the sheer fun of it! Yes, indeed, my daily planner is a very powerful motivational tool.

Probably the best daily plan that I've ever come across was written, some 50-plus years ago, by a lady called Sibyl F. Partridge. I recommend you keep and adopt this plan for yourself. Here it is:

Just For Today

1) **Just for today** I will be happy. This assumes that what Abraham Lincoln said is true, that "most folks are about as happy as they make up their minds to be." Happiness is from within; it is not a matter of externals.

2) **Just for today** I will try to adjust myself to what is, and not try to adjust everything to my own desires. I will take my family, my business, and my luck as they come and fit myself to them.

3) **Just for today** I will take care of my body. I will exercise it, care for it, nourish it, not abuse it nor neglect it, so that it will be a perfect machine for my bidding.

4) **Just for today** I will try to strengthen my mind. I will learn something useful. I will not be a mental loafer. I will read something that requires effort, thought and concentration.

5) **Just for today** I will exercise my soul in three ways; I will do someone a good turn and not get found out. I will do at least two things I don't want to do, as William James suggests, just for exercise.

6) **Just for today** I will be agreeable. I will look as well as I can, dress as becomingly as possible, talk low, act courteously, be liberal with praise, criticise not at all, nor find fault with anything and not try to regulate nor improve anyone.

7) **Just for today** I will try to live through this day only, not to tackle my whole life problems at once. I can do things for twelve hours that would appal me if I had to keep them up for a lifetime.

8) **Just for today** I will have a programme. I will write down what I expect to do every hour. I may not follow it exactly, but I will have it. It will eliminate two pests, hurrying and indecision.

9) **Just for today** I will have a quiet half-hour all to myself and relax. In this half-hour sometimes I will think of God, so as to get a little more perspective into my life.

10) **Just for today** I will be unafraid, especially I will not be afraid to be happy, to enjoy what is beautiful, to love, and to believe that those I love, also love me.

Isn't that a wonderful piece? Nevertheless, please don't simply read it and be entertained by it. Instead, adopt it as your own plan of action. You see, when you have a plan you have something to focus on, you have a vision, an understanding of how things will be. This gives you hope and inspiration. It gives you the motivation to get into action and do something. Without a plan you don't have any of this, instead you just have wishful thinking that things will turn out all right in the end! The book of Proverbs puts it rather more candidly:

"Where there is no vision, the people perish." (Proverbs 29:18, KJV)

Daily planning, then, gives you vision and the motivation to get into action. Have you noticed that the word 'motivation' is a shortened version of the words, 'motive-in-action'? Simply put, without a plan or a vision there is no motive and no motivation.

On a similar note regarding this subject of having vision, there was an experiment conducted recently on rats to test their ability to survive under stress. One rat was placed into a container of water in a room which was then made devoid of all light. The rat swam for some three minutes before giving up. Denied of light and not able to see anything, it surrendered to hopelessness. Another rat was then placed in the same situation, except that this time a tiny beam of light was allowed to filter into the room. The second rat swam for almost a day and a half (nearly 36 hours) before giving up! The ray of light gave it hope (albeit false hope), which motivated the rat to continue in its struggle. Now I certainly do not condone such experiments on animals; however, I share this example with you to prove the point. Having something to focus on inspires and motivates you into taking action.

In summary, then, if you want to find daily inspiration, become an avid subscriber to the idea of a daily planner or a 'things-to-do' list. Remember, when you have a plan you have something to focus on, and something to inspire you.

2. *Get into action*

Having a list or a plan to work from may be inspiring but, of course, you have to physically get to work for the plan to actually succeed. Remember Thomas Edison's quote: "Genius is one per cent inspiration and ninety-nine per cent perspiration." The second thing, then, is to force yourself from inertia to action. Let me put it like this: "If your get-up-and-go has got-up-and-gone then get up and go after it!" Sometimes you just have to start where you are and then, as I said earlier, the motivation will eventually catch up to you. In any event, you were meant to work, not to sit around watching and waiting all the time. A human being should always be a human doing. Remember again, the words of Napoleon Hill:

> "Do not wait. The time will never be just right. Start where you stand, and work with whatever tools you may have at your command, and better tools will be found as you go along."

Just jump into action, be bold, take a leap of faith and the motivation will catch up with you before you know it.

This is what happens to young eaglets when they learn to fly: they jump into action and take a leap of faith. Well, actually, they are usually forced into action! Maybe you'll have heard the phrase, 'stirring up the nest'? This relates to stirring up a bees' or wasps' nest but it could just as easily refer to what happens when it's time for the eaglets to learn how to fly. You see, for several weeks the eaglets have sat around watching and waiting, and also being waited upon hand and foot, as it were, by the parent birds. But finally the time comes for the offspring to leave the nest and the issue for the parents then becomes how to inspire them to do so. Well, this is where they are given a helping hand (or wing)! One day the mother bird senses the time has come, so she stops feeding the eaglets. Of course, this makes them very eager! Next she begins to demolish the nest, literally tearing away great chunks at a time and letting them fall to the ground. This makes the eaglets very uncomfortable! Finally, now that they are hungry and homeless, the eagle flies to a nearby perch and calls to her offspring to come. It doesn't take long for them to get the message! Sooner, rather than later, they take their leap of faith and begin to fly!

Sometimes, you have to push yourself (or others) into action. It's like drawing water from a well: you have to prime the pump (expel the air) and then apply force before the water flows freely. Likewise, sometimes you have to force inspiration to flow before it will flow freely. I know this, all too well, from my own writing. Sometimes I have to force myself to start. In fact, some anonymous but like-minded author once said, "Inspiration is the act of drawing up a chair to the writing desk." That's very true. It is also paradoxical in that inspiration happens when you get into action and 'inspire' it to happen! So then, get into action, and don't allow others to put you off. There will always be people who try to do this, but don't listen to them. Don't allow them to pull you down or keep you back. Instead, take the lead and just remember this: those who don't make dust eat dust!

Here's one of my favourite inspirational verses. Again, unfortunately, the author is lost to me, but let this verse inspire you to get into action anyway:

> People are unreasonable, illogical and self-centred;
> Love them anyway.
> If you do good, people will accuse you of selfish, ulterior motives;
> Do good anyway.
> If you are successful, you will win false friends and true enemies;
> Succeed anyway.
> Honesty and frankness will make you vulnerable;
> Be honest and frank anyway.
> The good you do today will be forgotten about tomorrow;
> Do good anyway.
> Big people with big ideas can be shot down by little people with small minds;
> Think big anyway.
> People favour the underdogs but follow only the top dogs;
> Fight for the underdogs anyway.
> What you spend years building can be destroyed overnight;
> Build anyway.
> Give the world the best you have and you'll get kicked in the teeth;
> Give it the best you've got anyway!

Moving on, now, I want to offer a word of warning about the dangers of apathy or indifference. Let me start by reminding you of what we discussed earlier (in Chapter 4); there is a human tendency to always seek the path of least resistance. We naturally prefer things to be easy and comfortable, and so we try to avoid any unnecessary bother. Unfortunately, inspiration rarely visits when you are being lazy or inactive, or when you are wallowing in your comfort zone, or when you are nonchalant about doing something. Simply put, you have to push yourself (and others) if you (or they) are to avoid the adversaries known as apathy and indifference.

You see, indifference has a sneaky habit of creeping up on you without being noticed, at least not in the beginning that is. Marriage, work, body weight, personal fitness, etc., it is never one major thing that brings a person to the realisation that he has become indifferent and has lost something, but an accumulation of lots of little things over a period of time. It's like the often-quoted story of the frog in the pan of water. Drop a frog into a pan of hot water and it will immediately jump out. But take a frog and pop it into a pan of cold water, then turn up the heat slowly until the water boils, and you end up with a cooked frog! Like I said, indifference creeps up on you.

So then, to find inspiration, push yourself and don't allow obstacles, or people, or excuses, or lack of whatever you need, to stop you from making a start. Don't succumb to complacency and don't get caught out by apathy or indifference. Just get into action. Let me say it again: begin where you are and do the very best you can, and before you know it, inspiration will catch up with you. As Bob Gass says,

"The longest road in the world is always shorter once you make your first step."

Step out then, and get into action.

Finally, before signing off, I want to say a word or two about inspiring others. Did you know that the best way to inspire people is to catch them doing something right? In other words, to encourage them, offer praise or a pat on the back. John Maxwell puts it like this:

"Man does not live on bread alone; sometimes he also needs a little buttering up."

Everyone needs encouragement occasionally. Everyone needs feedback. Everyone needs to feel that they are, in some way, significant; people need to know that their contribution counts, whatever that contribution may be. Without some significance and encouragement life would be worthless. As Samuel Johnson wrote back in 18th century England:

"The applause of a single human being is of great consequence."

Why? Because we, as human beings, have a deep-down desire to be appreciated. We want to know that our efforts are worthwhile; we want to feel wanted, accepted, well-liked and loved. So it is, that when someone stops to acknowledge us and they offer a few encouraging words of praise, we are inspired to further effort.

So, whether it be your child, spouse, employee, subordinate, friend or even your boss, be a 'good-finder'. Make a difference to the people you meet and especially to the ones who are close to you. Offer a word or two of encouragement, support them, urge them on and let them know that you appreciate them.

Go on, inspire them – and yourself!

Yours cordially,
Uncle Bob

Chapter Nine

Beware the Dirge of Discontent

*Let thy discontents be thy secret – if the world
knows them 'twill despise thee and increase them.*
Benjamin Franklin

Dear _ _ _ _ _ _ _ (fill in your name),

It always seems to be the case, for me at least, that whenever I prepare material for a speech or begin to write about a specific subject, I am affected by the subject matter somehow. For example, if I am writing about having a positive attitude or faith, then the odds are pretty good that my own attitude or faith will be tested, or else I will glean a fresh understanding of the topic or have a revelation about it. In other words, I experience afresh that which I am writing about. This is nothing new, of course, and a lot of people encounter the same thing. For example, many professors preparing a lecture or preachers preparing a sermon will go through a new learning experience themselves. They often gain as much insight as most of their audience, if not more.

This letter is no exception and when I set out to begin writing it I had, as usual, an encounter with the subject matter – discontentment! For a full day I seemed to be afflicted with 'the dirge of discontent'. It was as though I had a spirit of dissatisfaction hovering about me and, let me tell you, I was a real GROUCH! I'm afraid that I found myself complaining about anything and everything. In fact, I am ashamed to admit that I was a grumbling, quarrelsome sour-puss! Needless to say, it was not a pleasant experience and I'm extremely glad that it's over. (Believe me, I shan't be in any hurry to revisit this subject!)

After hearing my disgraceful (for an attitude trainer) confession, let me now ask you a question or three. Have you been a grouch recently? Do you feel dissatisfied with your circumstances or utterly discontented with your lot in life? Have you ever felt completely fed up and cheesed-off with everyone and everything? Yes? Well, guess what? You're not alone! We all have such feelings from time to time, every last one of us (some more often than others, of course). That much is plain fact! But here's another fact: if all you can do is grouch and complain and dwell on what is not right or what you haven't got – rather than on what you have got – then you will always be discontented. Always! Let me put it this way: if you focus only on the negative elements in your life, then all you are ever going to get is negative responses and results.

Back in 1921, Dr Russell H. Conwell wrote a short , simple essay, which demonstrates this point. The essay started out as a lecture in psychology, which was originally delivered before the Yale College of Law, Connecticut, USA. So popular was its message that Dr Conwell went on to deliver the lecture over 4,000 times. The revenue generated from people paying to listen to Russell Conwell deliver this speech soon shot past a million dollars – money that was used to finance a new learning facility called Temple University. Today, almost 80 years later, the essay or lecture is still available but now as a small book – a best-seller in its own right – and with the same title as the original lecture: *Acres of Diamonds*. I highly recommend this book to you and urge you to read it for yourself. Here's my version of the opening story.

A Persian farmer by the name of Al Hafed once lived by the shores of the Indus River. Hafed was a wealthy and contented man. He had money, a large, productive farm and a beautiful wife and family. It seemed he had everything. Then one day a priest visited Hafed and that night by the fire, told him stories about how God had made the world. The priest told Hafed that in the beginning the world was just a great bank of fog high up in the heavens. God caused the fog to swirl around in circles, increasing its speed until it became a vast ball of fire. Then, as it slowed and cooled, the mass condensed and moisture formed upon the surface or outer crust and cooled it more quickly. The inner crust, however, remained molten and in places this molten interior would erupt through the outer membrane, causing hills and valleys and mountains to be formed. Depending upon the speed at which these molten eruptions cooled, granite was formed, then copper and, if it cooled more slowly, silver, gold and finally, diamonds!

The priest told Al Hafed all about diamonds and how, with a diamond the size of a penny, he could buy several properties like his own. The priest told him that with a handful of similar diamonds he could practically buy the country and with his own diamond mine he could command influence and power the world over. Alas, when Hafed retired to bed that evening he had become a poor and discontented man.

The next morning, Hafed beseeched his visitor to tell him where he could find diamonds for himself. The priest replied that diamonds were always found in the white sands of rivers that flow down from the valleys between high v-shaped mountains. Shortly afterwards, Hafed sold his farm and all of his belongings and set off on his quest to discover diamonds. He travelled far and wide and searched long and hard for many years, but was never able to find so much as a single gemstone. Eventually, when he had spent everything he had and was completely destitute, he threw himself into the sea and drowned himself.

The story, however, is not finished there. One day, the old farmer who bought Hafed's land was watering his camels at the creek that ran through his fields. As he waited for his animals to drink their fill he noticed a shimmering light bouncing up at him from a fractured stone by the water's edge. He picked up the dark stone and marvelled at the hidden beauty twinkling from the fracture. He took the piece of rock home and placed it on his shelf as an ornament.

Some time later the old priest returned to the farm and was invited inside to refresh himself. At once he saw the ornament and exclaimed in an excited voice, "A diamond! – Hafed, has he returned?"

"Oh no." replied the farmer somewhat bemused, "That's just a worthless rock I found in the creek."

The priest asked the farmer to show him exactly where he had found the rock and the farmer led him out into the fields. There in the white sands of the creek, which flowed in from a valley between high v-shaped mountains, they found another diamond and another and another. And so it was that the Golconda diamond mines of

India were actually discovered. There were literally 'acres of diamonds', making it one of the richest mines in history.

The story of Hafed is true to life for a lot of people. If we would just stop to think, most of us would see that we have a great deal to be thankful for. But if, like Hafed, you become entirely focused on what you don't have, you often lose even that which you do have. Let me say it again: if all you can do is grouch and complain and dwell on what is not right or what you haven't got, then you will always be discontent and you will never be truly happy.

Now don't misunderstand me: I am not, for one moment, suggesting that each of us should simply be content with our lot in life. Quite the opposite, in fact. We should never be content with staying as we are. Instead we should always be striving for improvement and personal development. So then, let me make it perfectly clear that for the purposes of this letter, there is a very significant difference between *not being content* with your lot and being discontented or disgruntled with your lot.

Obviously, prevention is always better than cure and so the best way to avoid discontentment is to never allow it to afflict you significantly in the first place. Easy said, I know, but let's now look at this in a little more depth.

Let me begin by quashing a popular misconception about the reasons why some people are more successful than others.

If I had $1 for each time I've heard, "It's all right for you, but my problem is different" ... In fact, if I had $1 for each time I've heard people wishing they were someone else or wishing they had what others have instead of what they themselves have ... Indeed, if I had $1 for each time I've heard the 'dirge of discontent' voicing excuses or 'reasons' why a person is not enjoying success, then I'd be a great deal richer!

There is a popular misconception that some people just don't have any problems, but that's not true: everyone has problems and most of them are probably far worse than yours and mine. As the late Dr Norman Vincent Peale used to say, "The only place in the world where people don't have problems is a graveyard!" Everyone has problems; it's just that some people learn to deal with them and some people don't. At the end of the day, this is just a matter of perspective. Like the story of two men looking out of the prison bars – one looked down and saw only mud, the other looked up and saw the stars – same surroundings just a different perspective.

Another popular misconception is that "some people have all the luck," but once again this is not true. You see, good luck is usually just what happens when preparation meets opportunity. In other words, some people prepare and look for opportunities, and thereby make their own luck!

Being disgruntled or discontented is what happens when you allow things to get out of focus; when you allow the everyday problems of life to become everyday, life-consuming problems! Discontentment often causes bitterness, resentment and self-pity. Remember what Zig Ziglar calls, 'The PLOM Syndrome' (Poor Little Old Me). Discontentment is like a debilitating disease breeding negativity and failure. In a nutshell, it blinds you, it holds you back and stops you from trying to get on and achieve. The lyrics to 'The Dirge of Discontent' are, "It's not fair," "If only..." "Why me?" and, "I wish things were different!" Sound familiar? Well, let's see about changing the lyrics to that song and, for that matter, the very tune itself.

Remember, everyone has problems, and therefore, everyone has to make a choice whether to dwell on them, disregard them or deal with them. Here's an old story to illustrate the point:

There was once a wise old ruler who became concerned about the unrest and discontentment of his subjects. His people were always moaning and complaining about something or other. It seemed that each had a 'cross' to bear and their dissatisfaction was beginning to consume them. The wise old king decided it was time to get things into perspective, so he invited his subjects to gather before him so that they could openly voice all of their problems, troubles and complaints.

Well, the people came from all around and a great crowd gathered before the king. Then, one by one, they began to share their tales of woe, each complaining of unfairness or ill-treatment or various problems with neighbours, work, family – griping about his or her condition and unfortunate circumstances. When eventually the last person had spoken, the wise king stood and gave his counsel. He suggested that each person should exchange his problem with one of his neighbours. A silence descended upon the court as each man contemplated the King's advice, and then a very strange thing happened. One by one, the people turned and began to walk away,

95

no longer discontented. For when the opportunity was presented to actually swap places with someone else, the people decided to keep their own problems and deal with them, rather than exchange them for new and unknown ones.

Think about it. Everyone has problems. Would you really want to swap yours for someone else's? Would you swap your job, your health, your finances, your children, your family? Really swap them? The fact is, life is tough and we all experience hard and difficult times. Certainly, everyone enjoys good times as well but, on the whole, life is not easy and not always fair. So then, instead of bemoaning your lot, doesn't it make more sense to grit your teeth and to get on with doing something about it? Doesn't it make sense to stop feeling sorry for yourself because of what you haven't got and instead, start to do something positive with what you have got and improve your situation? There's an old saying that goes, "I once had the blues because I had no shoes; but then upon the street I met a man who had no feet!" The message is loud and clear: you should count your blessings not your problems. Here's a poem I came across some time ago, which says much the same thing.

God, Forgive Me When I Whine

Today, upon a bus, I saw a lovely girl with golden hair,
I envied her, she seemed so happy – I wished I were as fair.
When suddenly she rose to leave, I saw her hobble down the aisle;
She had one leg and wore a crutch; but as she passed ... a smile!
Oh, God forgive me when I whine,
I have two legs. The world is mine.

I stopped to buy some sweets, from a lad who had such charm.
I talked with him, he seemed so glad – being late would do no harm.
And as I left he said to me, "Thank you. You've been so kind.
"It's nice to talk with folks like you. You see," he said, "I'm blind."
Oh, God forgive me when I whine,
I have two eyes. The world is mine.

Later, while walking down the street, I saw a child with eyes of blue.
He stood and watched the others play – he did not know what to do.
I stopped a moment, then I said, "Why don't you join the others, dear?"
He looked ahead without a word, and then I knew, he could not hear.
Oh, God forgive me when I whine.
I have two ears. The world is mine.

With feet to take me where I'd go,
With eyes to see the sunset's glow,
With ears to hear what I would know,
Oh, God forgive me when I whine.
I am blessed indeed. The world is mine.

Anonymous

Do yourself a favour; rid yourself of discontentment and develop an attitude of gratitude. Get things into perspective, focus on the positive not the negative and in so doing, you'll see that things are usually not all that bad. It's been rightly said that life is 10 per cent what you make it and 90 per cent how you take it! In other words – once again – it's not what happens to us, but how we react to what happens to us that makes the difference. It's not that you should just put up and shut up! It's not that you should simply accept your circumstances or situation but rather, you should accept that you have a choice in how you will react to any given situation and you also have the option to change things. John Maxwell says:

> "Life can be likened to a grindstone. Whether it grinds you down or polishes you up depends on what you are made of."

Well, let me tell you, you're made of unique stuff! There is no one in the whole world, not now or ever, who is exactly the same as you. You are the rarest of individuals and this rarity gives you value. You are most definitely worth polishing! So then, instead of dwelling on your problems and allowing them to overcome you, concentrate on finding the solutions and overcome them.

Thomas Edison was a man who mastered the art of doing this. When he failed in any of his experiments he would often say, "I'm not discouraged because every wrong attempt is just another step forward." What a great attitude to have!

Someone else with a great attitude, although maybe not (yet) as famous, is Phil Wall, a motivational speaker and head of a UK-based charity called Hope HIV. Before pursuing this calling, Phil Wall was a police officer in London for eight years. He tells the story of how, during his time as a police officer, he reached the depths of despair, otherwise known as rock bottom!

One night, while off-duty, he was enjoying a meal in a hotel with his wife when suddenly the fire alarm went off. Assuming it was either a false alarm or a fire drill, he decided to continue with his meal and not be put off by the commotion around him. A few minutes later they began to smell smoke and figured it was time to leave! Then a man with a towel wrapped around his waist burst into the hotel foyer carrying a child in his arms and screaming that there were still two other children left upstairs. Phil, having learnt the whereabouts of the two children, ran up the smoke-filled stairs to try and save them. But by the time he reached the first-floor landing he was out of breath and so, inadvertently, he inhaled the acrid smoke. As he coughed uncontrollably he breathed in yet more smoke and began to choke. He now had to make an awful decision; in his own words, "I knew that if I kept going I'd asphyxiate and wouldn't get out alive, and if I turned around two small children might die!"

Well, Phil made the only decision he could. He himself lived to tell the tale, but that night, to his very deep regret, two small children under the age of nine tragically died. He had tried to rescue them but had failed!

That incident happened more than 10 years ago but the memory of it will live with Phil Wall forever. For a long time, the events of that evening haunted him and weighed him down, but eventually he began to realise that nobody could, nor ever would, say to him, "You shouldn't have tried," or "Don't ever try to do anything like that again."

Today, through his charity work at Hope HIV, Phil dedicates his life to helping and saving the lives of impoverished and orphaned children in Third World countries. The self-evident truth, and his personal axiom, is: "Failure can paralyse us to impotence or propel us to performance." Think about it.

Don't let failure or discontentment paralyse you to impotence, don't throw in the towel and quit. Instead, determine to get back on your feet again; resolve to climb back into the ring and fight another round. Just keep plugging away and don't let yourself be discouraged. Remember, "It's normally the last key in the bunch that opens the lock!"

On the next page are two ideas to help you overcome the doom and gloom of failure or discontentment.

1. Try this little exercise to give yourself an instant boost of happiness and appreciation for what you have. Visualise for a moment being completely destitute. Imagine that you have lost everything: your family, loved ones, friends, your job, your home, your health and every material possession you own. Imagine, just for a moment, that everything you hold dear is lost to you. Hold this awful thought for ten seconds or so and imagine how you'd feel and how things would be. Now picture yourself waking up, as if from a bad dream, and having every single thing returned to you. Feeling better? Remember, then, when you are down and discontent, count your blessings not your problems!

2. Take a piece of paper and write down seven things that you want to be remembered for, as if you were writing your own obituary. Write down seven qualities or achievements or legacies, seven reasons why yours was (is) a life that mattered. This, then, is your mission statement and it must now become your life's work. From now on, each and every day of the week, make sure that you are working towards at least one of those seven things that you want to be remembered for. Remember, if your life has a focus it has a reason, a purpose. Discover your true potential; map out how you want your obituary to read and then be constantly working towards that ideal.

I said earlier that we should never be content with staying as we are; instead we should be always striving for personal development, improvement and growth. Now, that's not to say feeling content is bad, on the contrary it is good – very good – just so long as it's not complete contentment, i.e. there is no room for further improvement. You see, as soon as you stop growing you begin rotting – just like a vegetable, only slower! No one should ever be completely content and satisfied with their lot in life unless, that is, they are actually ready to give up their life!

Writing that last sentence reminded me of a great little verse all about persistence and not quitting on life. I couldn't resist the temptation of sharing it with you so you can find it over the page.

It's a Frog's Life

Two frogs fell into a can of cream,
– or so I've heard it told.
The sides of the can were shiny and steep,
the cream was deep and cold.
"Oh, what's the use?" said No. 1,
"'tis fate – no help's around.
Goodbye my friend! Goodbye sad world!"
And weeping still he drowned.
But No. 2, of sterner stuff,
dog-paddled in surprise.
The while he wiped his creamy face
and dried his creamy eyes.
"I'll swim awhile, at least," he cried,
– or so it had been said.
"It wouldn't really help the world,
if one more frog was dead."
An hour or two he kicked and swam,
not once he stopped to mutter.
But kicked and swam, and swam and kicked,
then hopped out – via the butter.

Anonymous

It's now time for me to hop off again (excuse the pun) but before I do, let me admonish you, once more, not to listen or succumb to the 'dirge of discontent'. Don't allow your problems to get out of focus and overwhelm you, don't accept that there is nothing else you can do, don't become bitter or resentful or feel sorry for yourself. Instead, count your blessings, focus on the positives, jump into action and keep plugging away. Sooner or later things will start to improve. The sun will shine again! Remember ... even through the thickest, darkest clouds the sun is always shining – it's just that sometimes you have to wait for the clouds to pass before you can see it again. Either that, or you have to climb up through the clouds! Keep climbing, my friend, and until next time, I remain as always,

Yours cordially,
Uncle Bob

Chapter Ten

Self-Esteem – the Real You

A diamond is just a piece of coal made good under pressure.
Anonymous

Dear _ _ _ _ _ _ _ (fill in your name),

We have now progressed some way together and so I want you to ask yourself this all-important question: who am I? By that I mean, who is the real you, the one hiding beneath the surface? Allow me to explain with this illustration. A little while ago, I conducted a sales training programme in St Petersburg, Russia. Whilst I was there, I purchased some genuine handmade Russian dolls as a souvenir for my children. You know the sort of thing; where one doll is hidden inside another doll, which is hidden inside another and so on. When all the outer layers have been taken off, you finally discover the one whole doll. All the others are just a careful disguise: they pretend to be the genuine article, the whole doll, when really they are not.

Similarly with you: the genuine article, the real you, is that person hiding behind the masks, the person hidden deep within your protective outer layers. The real you is the person who is revealed whenever you are alone and the masks come down.

You see, we all wear masks, we all put on an outward show to try and impress people and make them accept us and like us. But when you take these masks off, when you look deep down inside yourself, then the true self, the genuine article, the real you is revealed.

Ask yourself these questions then:

+ Who is the real you?

+ Do you like what you see?

+ Do you (most important of all) accept yourself for who you are?

Of course, you are never going to be perfect, but in order to succeed in life the answer to those questions must be yes. You must accept who you are, indeed, you must *like* who you are. Now, by saying you should accept who you are, that's not to say that you shouldn't continually strive for improvement. As I've said before, as soon as you stop growing you start rotting away! Rather, what I am saying is that you should accept yourself and not keep pulling yourself down.

In this letter, then, I want to help you to understand your true self, which is the essence of your being – who you are. I also want to reveal to you the secrets of self-acceptance so that you need never again suffer from an inferiority complex.

In asking the question, then – Who am I? – I want you to, first of all, understand that you are more than just your body, your outer shell. Whether you are slim and have a great physique or whether you are overweight and largely out of shape, realise that this is just your shell or mode of transport. It is simply a vessel or body that contains the real you. Of course, it goes without saying that you must look after your body so that it will serve you well, but when your life is finally over and you depart this world, your body will no longer be needed; it will be discarded and left behind. When this does eventually happen, however, the real you, your spirit, the very essence of your being, still remains! You are more than just a body, you are a person within a body.

Likewise, you are also more than your amassed knowledge and education. In fact, the chances are extremely high that you will never use most of what you have learnt anyway! You are more than your intelligence or IQ rating. You are also more than your family, friends and loved ones. Certainly, they are important to who you are and what you are about, but they are not the essence of the person who you actually are. They are themselves – you are you! You are also more than your work: again, it is important but your work is not who you are. If you stopped working tomorrow would you cease to exist? Of course not. So then, you are more than your work.

Similarly, you are more than your strengths and weaknesses, more than your possessions, accomplishments and achievements, more than your memories, future aspirations and goals. You are also more than what others may think of you, and you are, most definitely, more than just a number in the countless billions of people who have come before you, exist today and, indeed, are sure to come after you.

In a nutshell, you are more than all of these things, and let me also say this: in my belief, you did not just happen to be. You are not simply an accident or some fluke of nature. You have your own completely unique DNA code, which is your individual blueprint, your authenticity stamp. Yes indeed, you are one of a kind, a unique individual made up of a body, mind and soul. For myself and millions of others, all of this unequivocally points to order and purpose; it points to a creator with infinite intelligence far beyond our comprehension.

Consider for a moment that a grand piano has 240 strings on which beautiful melodies can be played. The tiny human ear, in comparison, has the equivalent of 24,000 strings, which enable us to hear those melodies. Consider that a television camera has some 60,000 electrical photographic components, which pick up images and enable the camera to 'view' the surrounding area. In contrast, the human eye has over 137 million similar elements. Likewise, a personal computer has several hundred feet of wiring and the capacity to store several billion pieces of information, while a human brain, on the other hand, is infinitely more powerful. In fact, it has been suggested that the capacity for our brain to process and store information is, literally, unlimited. I have also heard it said that if you unravelled a man's brain cells and placed them end to end, there would be enough to go around the world 25 times! Indeed, the human body is a remarkably complex design. You are a wonderful creation.

Scientists, generally, agree that man is set apart and superior to the rest of the animals. As I've said before, all animals possess survival instincts: that is, finding food, water and shelter, as well as having the instincts for self-preservation and procreation. We humans have the same basic instincts, but we have emotional and spiritual needs as well as the physical ones. We also possess the qualities of morality, self-worth, reason and creativity. Man is in himself a creator; as the Bible says, 'the Creator' made him in his own image.

So you see, whether or not you believe in God, you are, indeed, a complex and unique individual, in my opinion, made up of body, mind and soul. The evidence suggests that you were designed and created with intention and purpose in mind. You also have the ability to choose and make your own decisions. In other words, you have free will to do as you please and believe what you like. The French philosopher, Voltaire, expressed it like this:

"The life of man is like a game of cards. Each player must accept the cards dealt to him and then he alone must decide how to play them in order to win the game."

Going back to the piano again, one person tries to play a tune and gets nothing but discord; another glides effortlessly up and down the keys and gets nothing but harmony. It is not the piano that plays the tune; rather it is the person who has chosen to learn how to play. It is the person who plays the tune, not the piano. Likewise in life: it is not the obstacles, problems or limitations but the actual player who determines the final outcome.

Many folk compare themselves to others and then just give up, because they consider the competition too great. But understand this, we are each of us made differently. We all have different gifts and talents and, ultimately, we are the ones who must decide whether or not we will put them to use. We must decide whether we will play our hand or sit the game out!

Now, let me change tack for a moment and ask you a question. The following sequence represents a complete set of six letters. Read them aloud and note the letters carefully: A, B, C, E, F, G. Is anything missing? Most people, in fact the vast majority, will say the letter D. Why is this? Why does there have to be something missing? I said this was a complete set of six letters, so why do we look for something else? Why do we insist that there is something missing instead of just accepting what we have and getting on with life? My advice, then, is this: stop looking for something that is missing, stop looking at what you haven't got and instead, start focusing on what you have got and put those assets to work for you!

Our diversity as individuals is enormous, and in this diversity lies the key to individual success. As someone once said, "What kind of a world would this world be if everyone in it were just like me?" Well, it would be a very tedious and boring place, would it not? So then, make the most of your individuality and put your gifts and talents to work for you in some way – however large or small – each and every day. Again, don't bemoan what you haven't got, instead, accept yourself for who you are, and then appreciate and use what you have been blessed with.

Consider, for example, the hummingbird, of which there are 338 species. The Cuban bee hummingbird is actually the smallest bird in the world measuring only six centimetres and weighing just three grams. The hummingbird can fly upside down and is the only bird in the world that can fly backwards. Its specially designed flight muscles allow wing beats of between 38 and 78 times a second, and during courtship male birds can attain wing-beat frequencies as high as 200 times a second. Talk about excitement! Imagine being able to flap your arms 200 times a second! This amazing ability allows the bird to hover in mid-air as it feeds by licking nectar from a flower.

However, for all its agility and flexibility the hummingbird cannot fly for any great distance and it cannot soar or ride on the wind currents as other birds do. On top of this, the hummingbird's legs are not designed for walking and so it can't hop from branch to branch. Instead, it has to fly everywhere, even from one flower stem to the next. Now a question for you: does the hummingbird give up on life because of what he can't do or hasn't got? Of course not! The hummingbird simply makes use of the talents it has and it does so very effectively.

As a comparison, now consider the largest bird in the world, the ostrich, which can grow up to 2.4 metres in height and can weigh around 136 kilograms. Now, of course, the ostrich can't fly to escape predators but then it doesn't need to. Its legs are so powerful that it can run at speeds of up to 80 kilometres an hour and take strides of around 4½ metres long.

My point, again, is this: we are, each of us, different. We all have different strengths and weaknesses, we all have different gifts and talents, and we all have different likes and dislikes. It is certainly not wrong to want to change, or to desire to be like someone else, as long as whatever it is you seek does not cause you to neglect the attributes and gifts that you already possess.

In the final analysis you, as an individual, call the shots! You must take whatever you have and use it to the best of your ability. You make the decisions, you make the choices and you decide how you will react to any given situation. Some people, rather than accepting and working with what they have, become obsessed with wanting to change the hand they have been dealt. Instead of playing the game, as it were, they choose to abstain and end up complaining and wishing that things were different. Conversely, however, the winners in life are the ones who always take what they have and put it to work for them. Here is a piece of verse taken from a poem – an old favourite written by Myra B. Welch – which reinforces the point beautifully.

The Touch of the Master's Hand

'Twas battered and scarred, and the auctioneer
Thought it scarcely worth his while
To waste much time on the old violin,
But held it up with a smile.
"What am I bidden, good folks," he cried,
"Who'll start the bidding for me?"
"A dollar, a dollar," then, two! "Only two?"
"Two dollars, and who'll make it three?"
"Three dollars, once; three dollars, twice;
Going for three ..." But no,
From the room, far back, a grey-haired man
Came forward and picked up the bow;
Then, wiping the dust from the old violin,
And tightening the loose strings,
He played a melody pure and sweet
As a carolling angel sings.

The music ceased, and the auctioneer,
With a voice that was quiet and low,
Said: "What am I bid for the old violin?"
And he held it up with the bow.
"A thousand dollars, and who'll make it two?
"Two thousand! And who'll make it three?
"Three thousand, once; three thousand, twice;
"And going and gone," said he.
The people cheered, but some of them cried,
"We do not quite understand.
"What changed its worth?" Swift came the reply:
"The touch of the Master's hand."

Myra B. Welch

We are all like that old violin. We all have the potential for greatness, we all have ability and we all have our own unique talents and gifts – things that we are good at. In the sales industry this uniqueness is referred to as your USPs, your Unique Selling Points. Let me explain: there are many similar companies selling similar products to similar customers. The key to success in sales, therefore, is to concentrate on selling your USPs, your unique selling points or qualities. Similarly, then, with you. The key to your success is for you to concentrate on *using* your gifts and talents, your USPs. I put the emphasis on the word 'using,' because – like the old violin again – if you don't use your talents then life becomes meaningless and worthless.

So, then, seek out ways in which you can serve others and put your talents to use. I like what Cavett Robert says on this subject:

"We can believe in what we are doing and feel a permanent sense of fulfilment only if we are rendering a service to others."

In a similar vein, Charles Dickens wrote, "No one is useless in this world who lightens the burden of another." What better way to develop, nurture and maintain your self-esteem than in being of service to others?

Your self-esteem, your perception of who you are and what you are like, is very important. It plays a very significant role in determining your future. Think about it: can you name one happy and successful individual who has lousy self-esteem or a bad self-image? No? This is because success and good self-image go together hand in glove. Having a good self-image or high self-esteem is an absolutely essential ingredient for success.

For the most part, everyone knows this to be true, and yet so many people end up with poor self-esteem when this need never be the case.

You see, positive self-esteem is inherent. We are all born with seeds of greatness within us – different forms of greatness, maybe, but the same seeds nevertheless. Throughout early childhood our self-esteem is, hopefully, developed and nurtured through the praise of parents and others. But then as we grow and venture out into the wider world, we start to experience various knocks, setbacks, failures and rejections, all of which have an effect on our confidence and self-esteem. Some people are so adversely affected that the wind is taken out of their sails and they succumb to a life of mediocrity, or worse! Others, however, learn to rise above the adversities of life. They have – and continue to develop – high self-esteem.

We all understand that if a car is not serviced or maintained it will eventually become a wreck; a building that isn't maintained will become shabby and dilapidated and a body that is not exercised and fed correctly will become unfit and overweight. Similarly, then, with a person's self-esteem: if it is not maintained it will start to decline. In my earlier book, *Maximise Your Potential*, I listed 15 different ways to develop, nurture and maintain your self-esteem. Here are another five ideas. If you follow them I guarantee you will start to build your self-esteem and see yourself in a new and more positive light.

1. *The will to win comes from within – not from without*

Take an iron bar worth about $10 in value. Make horseshoes out of that same iron bar and they'll be worth about $100. If you remove the impurities from the iron, add carbon, and make steel needles, they'll be worth $4,000. And if you take the same metal and make balanced springs for precision watches they'll be worth $500,000. We are like that iron bar; we all start from the same humble beginnings. However, our own value or self-worth is not and should not be left for others to manufacture. We must make that decision ourselves.

Realise, then, that high self-esteem is 'more taught than caught' and, mostly, it is self-taught through self-acceptance and affirmations. Self-esteem is just that: esteem or regard for oneself. It is not so much how others esteem you but the way you regard yourself that really matters. In other words, it is your view that really counts; it is your esteem, your perception and this, at the end of the day, is also your choice. As Eleanor Roosevelt once said, "No one can make you feel inferior without your consent." Think about it.

So, then, instead of being overly concerned about the opinions others may have of you, start being more concerned with the opinions you have of yourself. Those people who are out to simply put on a show and try to impress others are usually the ones who come unstuck and are left feeling unfulfilled and empty inside. As in the children's story of the foolish king who paid heavily for an invisible suit of clothes, people see through falsehood eventually. Maybe you remember the tale?

One day a fine-looking tailor arrived at court for an audience with the king. The tailor told the king that he had travelled from distant lands where he had discovered a magical yarn so beautiful that only the wisest of people could actually see it. The king's vanity got the better of him and so he ordered the tailor to make him a suit of the finest clothes and agreed to pay him three bags of gold coins. Well, the tailor went away and some weeks later returned carrying a large box. As he opened the box, he mimed taking out this precious garment of the finest cloth covered with tassels and jewels. As he mimed holding the garment, he spoke with great articulation about how the magical qualities of the yarn allowed only the wisest of people to be able to see and touch the suit. And how anyone who was a fool would not actually be able to see the suit at all; it would be invisible to him. Well, the king couldn't see a thing but he wasn't going to admit to being a fool, so he took off his outer garments and tried the suit on. As he posed grandly in front of a mirror all of his attendants said how handsome and regal and wonderful he looked.

The king paid the tailor his three bags of gold coins and then set off on a procession through the streets to show off his new suit to the people. Of course, what everyone actually saw was the king in his underwear, but nobody would admit to this. In fact, everyone remarked how grand the king looked in his new suit and what a beautifully fitting suit it was! But just then a young boy climbed up a lamppost to see what all the fuss was about. With a shriek of laughter the boy shouted, "Ha! Look, the king is in his underwear." Then everyone saw the truth and they too started pointing at the king and laughing at his foolishness.

Let me say it again: the important thing is how you see yourself, not how others see you. In other words, the will to win comes from within – not from without. So then, stop being overly concerned about trying to make a good impression on the outside; stop worrying about the opinions others may have of you and, instead, start being more concerned with the opinions you have of yourself – your self-esteem that is.

2. *Beauty is only skin deep*

In today's society there is so much pressure to look good. We have designer clothes, costume jewellery and fashion shows; we have beauticians, make-up artists and health clubs where we can go to work out and look good (or bad). We also have hair transplants, diet pills, cosmetic surgery and special creams to help keep us looking young. Then, there are false nails, false eyelashes, false teeth and false hair (wigs). There are dyes to change the colour of your hair, tanning creams to change the colour of your skin and different coloured contact lenses to change the colour of your eyes, regardless of whether or not you need to wear glasses!

The media are constantly bombarding us with images of slim, beautiful women with dazzling smiles and strong, handsome men with six-pack stomachs. This is what society says we should all strive to be like. Indeed, this is what we all really *want* to be like. Yes! In today's society there is so much pressure to look good.

Now, I'm not about to say that this is all a load of old baloney and that it's wrong to want to look good. Far from it, in fact. Often if you look good you feel good, and this has a major impact on self-esteem and the personal drive for accomplishment. However, what I am about to suggest is a complete paradigm shift in the normal way of thinking. You see, I have never met a person yet who was entirely happy with the way he or she looked. That is to say, a person who honestly did not want to change a single thing about his or her appearance – not size, not weight, hair loss, crooked teeth, nasal hair, nose size or, for that matter, the size of any other body part! I'll say it again: I have never met a person who was entirely happy with the way they looked, a person who, if they had a magic wand, wouldn't change at least something about their physical appearance. Furthermore, I don't believe that such a person exists!

The saying, 'beauty is only skin deep,' is very true. Beauty *is* only skin deep and, therefore, good looks alone are a shallow means of comparing ourselves to others. On the inside, of course, we all *look* the same.

So, then, to increase your self-esteem I fully and wholeheartedly recommend that you look after your outward appearance, but to further increase your self-esteem I want you to look on the inside, not just the outside. I want you to consider your body for the magnificent, wonderful machine that it is – not just its outward appearance, not just the surface beauty but also the inner beauty. In fact, next time you are alone and you undress, stand in front of a full-length mirror and look at those parts of your body that you don't particularly like; the parts that maybe you have a hang-up about; the parts of your body that deflate your ego. Then, instead of focusing on these self-labelled 'negative' aspects of your anatomy, consider instead what the function of that particular area or body part is. For example, your thighs and legs might be on the large side but instead of getting a complex or being hung up about it, be thankful that you have legs that allow you to walk, run, dance, jump, tiptoe and wiggle your toes! In other words, focus on the positive not the negative. At the end of the day, if you are comfortable with the way you look – great; if you are not comfortable then decide to do something about it if you can – remember, though, beauty is only skin deep.

One final point. When it comes down to your appearance, understand this: of all the things you wear your expression is always the most important.

3. *Come back and finish what you started*

Back in 1978 Gladys Knight and the Pips had a hit single with the title, "Come back and finish what you started". I remember the song well, especially the title. Maybe you can recall the lyrics:

"Come back and finish what you started, don't leave me hanging on and on."

A great exercise for increasing your self-esteem is to do just that – go back and finish what you started. What am I saying? Simply this: somewhere in your mind there is an unwritten list of things that you have been meaning to do, jobs left unfinished, fiddly little annoyances that you intend to one day get around to sorting out, letters you've been meaning to answer, repairs or renewals you've been planning to do ... whatever. You know the sort of thing I'm talking about? The sort of things that clutter up your mind and your in-tray or bottom drawer, the sort of things that get on top of you and then weigh you down, the sort of things that tug at your self-esteem, saying, "You're disorganised, you're hopeless, you never finish what you set out to do, and you never see a job through to the end."

Well, here's what to do. Sit down and make a complete list of all those unfinished jobs; a list of all the things you need to do in order to bring you up to par. Most people, about a week before taking a holiday, will make up a list of all the things they need to accomplish and do before they leave. They then use this list as a plan of action to help bring themselves up to date and also ensure they avoid being overwhelmed in a deluge of things to do when they get back. Similarly, then, with you. Don't agonise, organise. Make up your list. Then simply set to and start ploughing through the list, either delegating the work or doing it yourself and ticking each item off as you go.

This technique achieves results. Firstly, in making your list you relieve your mind of the pressure to remember everything. Secondly, you create a plan of action and a target to aim for. And thirdly, you experience a wonderful sense of accomplishment each time you get to cross an item off your list. All this adds up to achievement and increased self-esteem; so start making your list straightaway.

4. *Endorsements of value*

Here is another way to build self-esteem both in others and yourself. This idea originated from a sad, but true-life, story told by a teaching nun, Sister Helen Mrosla, concerning one of her classes and especially a young man called Mark Eklund.

Sister Helen recalls a day of unrest within her classroom, when the students were getting cranky and bickering with each other. To stop matters getting out of hand she made each of them take some paper and write down the names of all the other students, leaving a space in between each name. She then instructed her class to think of the nicest thing they could say about each of their classmates and told them to write it down beside their name. When they had done so, Sister Helen collected the papers. She took a fresh piece of paper for each student, wrote their name on the top and transcribed on to it all the nice comments that the other pupils had written about them. When she handed the individual lists back to each of the students they were absolutely amazed. One even made the comment, "I never knew the others liked me so much."

Several years passed and the students moved on. Then one day Sister Helen received the shock news that Mark Eklund, one of the students who had taken part in the exercise years before, had been killed in action in Vietnam. Mark's parents asked Sister Helen and the rest of his old classmates to attend the funeral. Afterwards, as they gathered in the family home, Mark's father approached the nun and opening his wallet he produced a dog-eared, folded piece of paper. "We thought you might recognise this," he said, "It was found on Mark's body after he was killed." It was the piece of paper from years before, listing all the nice things that Mark's classmates had said about him. He had treasured it so much that he kept it with him always.

Seeing what had just happened Mark's old classmates began to gather around Sister Helen to thank her, especially for what she had done that day years before. Then, one by one, they began to open wallets and purses and produce their own lists. Some had them at home in a drawer or a diary or an album, but it seemed that every one of them had kept their precious lists. Sister Helen wrote, "All I could do was sit down and cry."

Can you imagine what such a list would do for your self-esteem, or that of your family, friends, employees or colleagues? This is also a great team-building exercise – creating endorsements of value for each other. I want to recommend that you follow Sister Helen's example and put this exercise to the test.

5. Overcome self-imposed limitations

Let me ask you this: if you knew categorically that you couldn't fail, what would you attempt to do? Now another question: so what's stopping you? More likely than not, your answer will come down to some self-imposed limitations. Lack of resources, money, time, qualifications, opportunities ... Either that or else your inner voice tells you that it won't work, or you're not capable, or the time is not right, and so you limit yourself and don't even try.

Some time ago the following experiment was undertaken at a marine aquarium. A savage barracuda was placed into a large tank of water. The tank was then partitioned down the middle with another piece of glass, and a mullet fish was placed into the other side of the tank. Immediately, the barracuda tried to attack the mullet, but halfway across the tank its onslaught was abruptly and painfully cut short by the wall of partitioning glass. The barracuda recovered and tried again and again but each time he bumped his snout against the glass. Eventually, the barracuda learnt that chasing mullet fish was a painful experience and so it gave up trying. A little while later the glass partition was removed, but the barracuda would still only swim up to the point where the barrier had been, then it would turn around and swim back again. The barracuda had conditioned itself to believe it could not succeed and so it gave up trying.

It is the same with a lot of people. The fact is, you can condition your mind to accept that you won't succeed – just like the barracuda – but, conversely, you can also condition your mind to overcome your self-imposed limitations and achieve success.

Consider this analogy: do you know how they teach dolphins to jump high out of the water and over a rope? The trainers start by putting the rope below the surface of the water and then every time the dolphin swims over the rope it gets rewarded, but every time it swims under the rope it gets nada, zilch. Of course, the dolphin soon learns to go over the rope every time and it continues to do this, as the rope is gradually lifted higher and higher out of the water. The trainers build up the dolphin's belief system, they encourage it to overcome any self-imposed limitations and to keep climbing higher.

Similarly, then, with you: you can condition your mind to overcome your self-imposed limitations and achieve success. How?

Well it's all down to the starving-the-bad-dog-feeding-the-good-dog routine again (refer back to Chapter 5). Remember, I said it's as though we have two dogs inside our head – a good dog and a bad dog – and both of them are constantly fighting for the same piece of meat: to control our thoughts and beliefs. What we must do is feed the good dog and starve the bad dog. In other words, use positive affirmations – say them with conviction – and starve the negative thoughts to death. In so doing, you will give yourself the courage to overcome your self-imposed limitations; and you will give yourself the inspiration to get up, get going and get achieving.

When it comes to developing and maintaining high self-esteem the greatest asset you can have is self-discipline. This is one of the topics I'll be covering in my next letter but for now, let me close with an amusing tale not unrelated to our current subject of self-worth.

Three businessmen were discussing the definition of success and what it would mean for them to feel that they had 'arrived'. The first one said, "I'd consider myself a success if I was summoned to 10 Downing Street, London, for a private consultation with the Prime Minister." The second chipped in, "My definition of success is to be called to Number 10 for a private meeting with the Prime Minister, then the telephone hotline rings during our discussion and the Prime Minister ignores it." Finally the third one gave his opinion: "No, you've both got it wrong! You're a success when you are in the middle of private talks with the Prime Minister, the hotline rings, he answers it and then says, 'It's for you!'"

Remember this: smiling increases your face value.

Yours with a smile, then,

Uncle Bob

Chapter Eleven

Your Very Good Health

*Life is like a coin; you can spend it on whatever
you want but you can only spend it once and there
are no refunds. Make sure you spend yours wisely.*

Dear _ _ _ _ _ _ _ (fill in your name),

A book devoted to personal development and success just wouldn't
be complete without some mention of maintaining a personal
health and fitness programme. After all, what good is it to learn all
about the secrets of achievement and success if you don't then
have your health to enjoy it?

So, then, following on from my last letter – where we looked at
developing and maintaining high self-esteem – it now seems fitting
to tackle this issue that is, literally, close to everyone's heart!

Now, let me state, straight up front, that it is not my intention in
this letter to take you on a guilt trip. Nor is it my intention to bully
you or nag you into doing something that you don't really want to
do. Having said that, I have yet to meet a person who was serious
about success who wasn't also serious about looking after their
health. What I will do, in this letter, is share some thoughts and
ideas, as well as some expert advice, to help and encourage you
to lead a healthy lifestyle. To assist in this endeavour, I want to set
out the four main areas that we shall be looking at:

1. Food
2. Exercise
3. Habits
4. Self-discipline.

Food for thought

I have a friend, Eileen, who is an author and a respected nutritionist. Eileen states that there are a great many people in our society who are digging their own graves with a knife and fork! In other words, it might be a slow process, but their eating habits are actually eating away at their health. As the old saying goes, "You are what you eat." Think about it. Whether we eat healthily or unhealthily, the choice is ours, but our bodies will always produce the corresponding results.

Conversely, it has also been said, "It's not always what we eat but sometimes what's eating us that causes many medical problems." This, again, is very true. Things like constant stress, holding grudges, persistent worrying and the like have caused many an ulcer, mental breakdown, case of high blood pressure, heart condition, etc. Indeed, we have already looked at the effects of some of these behaviours in previous chapters. For now, then, let us concentrate on the effect of food.

At a recent leadership conference I had the opportunity to see and listen to the UK's diet and fitness guru, Rosemary Conley, give a presentation titled, "How to Keep Fit and Healthy". It really was an excellent presentation, due much to the fact that Rosemary delivered it with some simple, easy-to-follow, guidelines.

Now if you are anything like me, the dietary information written on some food packaging may as well be written in Martian! I mean, I have absolutely no idea what emulsifiers, E numbers and the various obscurely named vitamins and additives are supposed to do for you. Furthermore, if I am honest, I don't particularly care! I just want to know that what I am eating is healthy food; by that I mean, food that is good for me to eat. Rosemary's advice, when it comes to the labelling on food packaging, is to pay particular attention to the number of calories and to the fat content per 100 grams of foodstuff.

It's not good to eat late at night because when you do so, you don't give yourself a chance to work off what you have eaten. (Your metabolism slows when you are resting.) Indeed, as someone once said, "To remain fit and healthy, eat breakfast like a king, lunch like a prince and dinner like a pauper." In other words, and contrary to many people's eating habits, it is better to eat early rather than late. However, when it comes to looking after our figures and keeping our weight under control, Zig Ziglar about sums it up with this home truth:

> "We have all chosen to be the weight that we are because we have never eaten anything unintentionally or by accident!"

Now, of course, it is not just the quality of food that we eat, but also very much the quantity, that counts. The amount of food that we eat determines the calories available to us. (A calorie being the unit of measurement used to express the energy value of food.) If we consume the right amount of food our weight will remain constant; if we consume more than we need we will put on weight; and if we consume less food than we need we will lose weight. Now, that's fairly obvious stuff, but how can we accurately judge the right quantity of food? The answer to that question is simple but not always easy to swallow (pun intended): we have to discipline ourselves to count the calories. In other words, just as we measure the amount of fuel that we put into our car, so we must also measure the amount of fuel (calories) we put into our other vehicle, our body.

Experts tell us that the average daily calorie consumption required for a woman is between 2000 and 2200 calories a day. For a man that figure rises to around 2700 calories a day. Now, these are average figures taken from across the board and daily consumption levels depend upon each individual person's metabolic rate (the rate at which the body burns up energy). For example, a large, muscular, 25-year-old man, 193cm in height, who works in the construction industry, will almost certainly have a far higher metabolic rate – and so will consume far more calories than, say, a slim, 167cm tall man who sits behind a desk in a bank all day. However, as a benchmark these figures are a good measure: for a woman, 2000 to 2200 calories a day and for a man around 2700 calories.

Now, our many bodily functions such as breathing, blood circulation, digestion, hair growth, cell replacement and so on, obviously use a supply of energy and, indeed, burn up more than just a few calories. In fact, it's been calculated that if we were to stay in bed all day and do absolutely nothing at all, the average woman would still need around 1400 calories a day, and a man between 1700 and 2200 calories, just to stay alive! The remainder of our daily intake of calories is then either used up in our daily activities or converted and stored away as fat, for a rainy day!

So, to put it plainly, if you want to lose weight you need to reduce your daily intake of calories so that your body will call upon your fat reserves to make up the deficit. (Of course, exercise greatly increases energy consumption, as we shall see in a moment.)

Now, when I say to lose weight you need to reduce your daily intake of calories, I do not mean you should starve yourself or miss out on meals. This is not conducive to sustained weight loss. You see, if we go without food then our body automatically goes into what Rosemary Conley calls 'famine mode'. In other words, the body says to itself that there must be a shortage of food so I had better conserve energy. The consequence of going without food is a reduction in the metabolic rate, i.e. the bodily functions slow down and so require less energy. It stands to reason, then, that losing weight (permanently) is nothing to do with going hungry or starving yourself, but everything to do with a maintaining a calorie-controlled diet.

Another thing Rosemary explained very well is the difference in the types of food we eat; namely carbohydrates, proteins and fats. Rosemary recommends that we only eat foods that have a 4 per cent fat content or less. She also tells of an experiment she was involved in while doing some work with a nutritional institute. Three volunteers were asked to wear a 'metabolic hood' which measures the metabolic rate of the body. Each volunteer was then given a meal so that the scientists could examine the effects the meal would have on each individual's metabolic rate. The first was given a meal of pasta, which is rich in carbohydrates. Immediately, the metabolic rate increased as the body got to work digesting the food and converting the carbohydrates into energy. The second was given a meal rich in protein (meat or fish, etc.) and again the metabolic rate increased, though not quite so quickly. Finally, the third volunteer was given a large quantity of chocolate to eat, which is a foodstuff very high in fat. Amazingly, this time the metabolic rate hardly changed at all! The fat, instead of being broken down quickly and used as an energy source, was broken down extremely slowly and then stored away as fat deposits for use another day!

The experiment conclusively showed that the body breaks down and converts carbohydrates and protein easily and quickly, but with foods containing a high level of fat it does not. The lesson for all of us here is this: we should eat plenty of carbohydrates and proteins but have little to do with foods high in fat.

Now, these writings are not the place to get involved in giving detailed nutritional information but there are two very important points that I need to make perfectly clear. First, there is a very major difference between the carbohydrate from sugar and refined flour and the carbohydrates from unrefined, wholegrain foods. Suffice it to say, here, that unrefined or wholegrain foods are by far the better option. Second, in suggesting that you have little to do with foods that are high in fat, I don't mean you should avoid fats altogether. The fact is, some fats are essential to good health. In fact, my nutritionist friend, Eileen, tells me that some people have cut so much fat from their diet that they have actually ended up with poor health. Things like olive oil, oily fish and sunflower seeds are all rich in fats that are absolutely vital for good health and metabolism, and which also help to actually reduce harmful cholesterol.

Going back to Rosemary Conley, she compares carbohydrates to cash in your pocket or purse, which never seems to last very long, i.e. it is used up quickly. Proteins are like your salary, which is paid into your bank account every month; this is also spent quickly and pays for things like your mortgage or rent and general living costs. Fats, on the other hand, are like gold bullion stored away in secure vaults. In other words, they are not easily converted or spent. They are security for times of shortage.

When it comes to diet I am no expert, but one thing I do know: the key to healthy eating is balance, i.e. all things in moderation. Before we move on, let me just say one last thing about diet. It doesn't matter if you occasionally go all out and stuff yourself silly on chocolate and fresh cream cakes! Why? Because you can't put weight on that quickly. Just as weight creeps on, so it also creeps off. So, if your diet goes to pot one day, if you succumb to temptation and binge, then don't give up permanently; don't say dieting doesn't work, don't be too harsh on yourself. Just get back into action; set yourself a new target, a new goal and then get back with the programme.

To summarise this first section, then, here are some dos (rather than don'ts):

◆   Do be aware of what you eat; remember, plenty of unrefined carbohydrates and proteins

◆   Do avoid eating between meals

◆   Do eat your evening meal as early as you can

◆   Do drink a large glass of water before each meal (it fills you up, aids digestion and helps to transfer nutrients around the body more efficiently)

◆   Do eat more fruit (remember, an apple a day keeps the doctor away)

◆   Do have smaller servings

◆   And, yes – although I hate to be a killjoy – do avoid chocolate, biscuits, cakes and pastries.

If you want to lose weight then you have to reduce your calorie intake and stay away from high-fat foods. Remember, Rosemary Conley recommends choosing foods with under 4 per cent fat!

I know that's hard, and although I always strive to practise what I preach, I don't mind telling you that I struggle with this issue just as much as anyone else. My wife, Suzanne, will tell you that I am a sweet man (meaning that I like my desserts); and the fact the she is a great cook is a constant battle for me. Having said that, Suzanne always promotes the healthy, low-fat, alternatives – my problem is in wanting to go back for seconds and thirds! However, to strengthen my resolve I have a couple of little ditties I use, which go like this:

◆   "It's better to put it in the waste than on the waist" – or

◆   "It's better to put it in the bin than on my chin!"

I want to recommend that you adopt this policy in your own life. You see, diet is one of those areas that you have to work on continually throughout your entire lifetime, but there again, as someone once said, "If you are not working on yourself then you're not really working."

Exercise

Of course, apart from diet another great way to ensure weight loss – and keep in shape – is to increase your personal expenditure of energy consumption. In other words, to exercise. Now, I'm fully aware that time is one of the biggest constraints on taking regular exercise, but the fact is, as I have said before, those people who say they cannot afford the time to exercise are the ones who particularly can't afford *not* to find the time!

Exercise – regular exercise that is – is just as important to personal development and success as getting out of bed in the morning! Benjamin Franklin said it best with these words:

> "Keep thy shop and thy shop will keep thee."

I said in the beginning of this letter that I wasn't going to bully you, but – if you don't already exercise – I've changed my mind! Some people only respond to heavy-handed tactics, and some people only become concerned about their health when they haven't got it anymore, or there is a threat of losing it. Think about it. The graveyards are full of rich, 'successful' men and women who died before their time because they literally ran themselves into the ground – six feet under, that is! Indeed, as author Wesley Harris writes:

> "Some people take more care of their car than of their body."

Someone else said:

> "Others take more care of their pets than they do themselves. Their animals can run like the wind and yet they themselves can barely make it up a flight of stairs."

Now, practically everyone has insurance of some kind or another. We insure our cars, our home and our belongings. We have medical insurance, travel insurance, life insurance. Why is it, then, that so many people neglect to help insure their future by exercising? Mostly, the answers to that question are: no desire; no fear of the consequences of not doing it; no time; lack of discipline; and bad habit patterns. We shall be looking at how to overcome these later but for now, understand that change will only happen when you want it badly enough. Let me put it like this: the key to willpower is want-power! The following little rhyme about sums it up.

I spent a fortune on a trampoline,
A stationary bike and a rowing machine.
Complete with gadgets to read my pulse,
And gadgets to prove my progress results,
And others to show the miles I've charted;
But they left off the gadget to get me started!

When it comes to finding the time for regular exercise there is a popular misconception that a person has to commit several hours a week to a dedicated fitness programme. Now, whilst this is always the best option it is not necessarily the only option. You see, exercising can be just as effective as a daily ongoing thing as it is as a regular, but periodic thing. Let me explain. You don't necessarily have to go jogging, or go to the gym or swimming pool or football oval or whatever, in order to exercise effectively. You can also exercise at your desk, workstation, home or even whilst doing your chores. Here are a dozen tips, a list of exercise techniques that you can employ everyday to help you keep fit and mobile and also to help burn off extra calories – calories that, maybe, you wouldn't otherwise use up.

1. Don't sit if you can stand, don't stand if you can walk, don't walk if you can run.

2. Don't drive if you can cycle or go by foot.

3. Always take the stairs instead of the lift.

4. If you have a two-storey house,when you are at home, instead of piling things up on the bottom of the stairs to take up later, take them up straightaway. Better still, take them up one item at a time.

5. Constantly suck in your stomach. This exercise not only gives you better posture, but it also makes you look taller, helps to prevent back problems and burns up more calories.

6. Instead of trying to find a carparking space as close as you can to the office, park at the far end of the carpark and walk. (If it's raining, run!)

7. Similarly at the supermarket: park at the far end of the carpark and, if you are able to do so, carry your shopping back to the car. If there is too much, use a shopping trolley but make sure you take the trolley back to the furthest bay when you have finished with it!

8. Take the batteries out of the remote control and move your chair further away from the television set.

9. Do leg exercises as you sit watching TV.

10. Whenever you walk anywhere, do so as though you are on an important mission. In other words, don't amble along; walk briskly.

11. Get yourself a dog!

12. When you do the housework, mow the lawn or clean your car, again, do so vigorously and make sure you stretch and bend this way and that.

To sum up, make exercise a habit – no, more than that, make it a life attitude. If you treat exercise as an obligation or a burden, then it will always be hard work. But if you treat exercise as a game, a fun thing to enjoy at every possible opportunity; indeed, if you look for opportunities to exercise, then it will become easy and enjoyable. At the end of the day, the decision is yours.

At this point, let me give you a word of warning: taking things to the extreme is not good for you. I'm a member of a gym and I visit two or three times a week for a general workout. But there are some people who go every single day and for many hours at a time: they are 'body worshippers,' fanatical about their fitness, diet and, especially, their appearance! It seems that most of their time is spent making themselves look good on the outside. Whilst this, in itself – looking good – is not wrong, it is definitely not wise to be so obsessed with one's appearance, which is, after all, only your outer casing or shell.

I'm reminded here of an analogy I once heard about a man who bought his girlfriend an expensive diamond ring. The jeweller gift-wrapped the ring free of charge in a beautiful, ornate box, tied it together with a red ribbon and had it personally delivered to the lady's home. The next day when the man called for her, she said,

"Sweetheart, what a beautiful box you sent me. It's so pretty and delicate; I promise to always keep it wrapped up and safe so that no harm will ever come to it!" Rather a ridiculous scenario, don't you think? Yet no more ridiculous than those individuals who spend all of their time and efforts on their bodies – their outer casings – especially if they neglect the more valuable matters on the inside, to do with the heart, mind and soul.

Let me say it again, taking things to the extreme is not good for you. The rule of thumb should always be 'balance' and this leads us nicely on to our final points.

Habits and Self-Discipline

Have you ever done one of those puzzles where you have to guess the missing word using the first letters from each of the answers to the clues? Well, here's a similar puzzle, but in this one you don't need to find any letters, just try and work out what is being described. See if you can guess what or who it is.

> I am your constant companion.
> I am your greatest helper or your heaviest burden.
> I will push you onward or drag you down to failure.
> I am completely at your command.
> Half the things you do, you might just as well turn over to me,
> And I will be able to do them quickly and correctly.
> I am easily managed; you must merely be firm with me.
> Show me exactly how you want something to be done,
> And after a few lessons I will do it automatically.
> I am the servant of all great men
> And, alas, of failures as well.
> Those who are great, I have made great.
> Those who are failures, I have made failures.
> I am not a machine, though I work with all the precision of a
>   machine,
> Plus the intelligence of a man.
> You may run me for profit, or run me for ruin;
> It makes no difference to me.
> Take me, train me, and be firm with me,
> And I will put the world at your feet.
> Be easy with me and I will destroy you.
> Who am I?
>   *Author Unknown*

Have you guessed it yet? The answer is 'HABIT'. Now go back and read through the passage again, but this time recognise the truth behind each statement and realise just how powerful our habits are.

Horace Mann (1769–1859), the so-called 'father of America's education system,' observed that:

> "Habit is a cable; we weave a thread of it each day, and at last we cannot break it."

Take a thin piece of fuse wire and you can snap it easily, but take several strands and twist them together and it's a very different story. Our habits are formed like that, both good habits and bad habits; one strand at a time or one routine or action repeated constantly until a strong cable – an accepted behaviour – is formed.

Good habits for diet and exercise are formed one day at a time. They start out as good intentions or thoughts. When the thoughts are persistent enough they gain power and energy, enough to move a person into taking action; repeated actions then become habits; habits develop character and character builds a person's future. It all starts at the point when you put your good intentions into action. So, whatever good habit you want to develop, whether it's in order to lose weight, get fit, become better educated or whatever else, be self-disciplined enough to start today and just take it one step at a time. It doesn't matter how big the rock in front of you is; if you just keep chipping away, in the end it's going to break. First of all, though, you have to start; you have to begin chipping away!

Now, if you read this and say to yourself, "That's it! Ian's right – and I'm 'gonna' get started," then good for you, because winning starts with beginning. However, let me warn you that in the beginning it is going to be hard work, maybe even very hard work! A lot of people start off well enough but then the drag of the outgoing tide (the old behaviour) pulls them back into familiar waters! Someone once put it like this:

> "A bad habit is like a warm bed: easy to get into and hard to get out of!"

This is where your self-discipline comes into play.

Discipline is one of those characteristics common to all winners in life. It is a characteristic based on patience, restraint, self-control and determination. Formidable-sounding qualities, but self-discipline is not really that difficult. You see, self-discipline is nothing more than the exercising of a few small disciplines every day. It is the compound effect of these disciplines, repeated every single day, that eventually leads to success. The fact is, you don't have to do that much to make a considerable amount of difference in a fairly short period of time. A few daily disciplines can make a big difference over a period of a month, a major difference over three months and a colossal difference over a year. It's like asking the question, "How do you eat an elephant?" The answer is, you eat an elephant one bite at a time! Similarly, when it comes to exercising self-discipline, the key to success is one day or one bite at a time. Just make sure you take a big enough bite! By that I mean, make sure that the action you take has an effect. Let me give you an analogy. During Prohibition in the United States in the 1920s, the American Congress ruled that any substance containing less than 1 per cent alcohol was non-intoxicating. In other words, anything less than 1 per cent was considered ineffectual – it didn't matter or make the slightest bit of difference. So then, make sure that your few daily disciplines require enough effort to make a difference.

You can do it if you put your mind to it. You can lose weight, you can get fit, you can develop a healthy lifestyle and you can turn back the clocks if you are willing to endure the pain of discipline. In any event, everyone must endure one of two pains: either the pain of discipline or the pain of regret. At the end of the day, as I said earlier, that decision is yours. I trust you will make your decisions wisely.

Well, that's about all for now so until next time, cheers, and your very good health.

Yours cordially,
Uncle Bob

Chapter Twelve

Dare to be Different

If you want to lead the orchestra you have to be willing to turn your back on the crowd.
Anonymous

Dear _ _ _ _ _ _ _ (fill in your name),

I recently heard about an experiment conducted on some teenagers to study the effects of peer pressure. The experiment was set up to see whether or not a child would run with the crowd, even when he or she knew it was wrong to do so, or whether the child would dare to be different. The actual source of the test eludes me but the findings do not make for happy reading.

This is briefly what happened. Some examiners staged an exercise in a school with a group of ten teenagers, supposedly to test their eyesight. The examiners told the whole group that they would hold up some cards with three lines on them – lines 'A,' 'B' and 'C' – and each line would be of different length. All the students had to do was to raise their hands when the examiner pointed to the longest line. However, the examiners had secretly instructed nine of the students beforehand to deliberately give the wrong answer so that they could observe what the tenth would do. They were told to vote for the second longest line. (The tenth had no idea that the other nine were colluding against him.)

When the first card was held up, it was apparent that line 'C' was longer than the others, but when the examiners pointed to line 'A' (the second largest line) nine hands immediately shot into the air. The tenth teenager hesitated for a moment, glanced at his classmates and then also raised his hand. The examiners tried again with another card and as before nine hands were immediately raised supporting the wrong answer. Again the tenth student hesitated slightly but followed suit and also raised his hand. This happened time and time again with the same result each time.

Afterwards, the examiners revealed to the teenager in question what had happened and they asked him why he had deliberately answered incorrectly. The young man replied that on the first occasion he had assumed that he had misheard the question and so he had followed the example set by his classmates. The second time around, he said that he realised the others had answered incorrectly but he didn't want to attract attention to himself and so, even though he knew it was the wrong answer, he went along with them. Eventually he admitted to the examiners that he had continued along this path because he considered it more important to go along with the others and 'fit in' rather than stand alone and be right! The depressing thing is that he was not the only one. In fact, nearly 80 per cent of the teenagers tested behaved in a similar fashion. Like I said, the findings do not make for happy reading!

Many adults act in a similar way: they go along with the crowd and do as everyone else seems to be doing, or else they remain inactive or silent, even when they know that their actions – or inactions – are not quite right. Many simply don't want to make waves or rock the boat and so they go along with things, looking for an easy life. Instead of daring to be different, or making a stand and doing what they know is right, they choose to be unconcerned, they choose to blend into the background and not be bothered.

As human beings we don't want to be alienated. In fact, we all have the innate desire to 'belong' or to run with the crowd – this is known as the 'herd instinct' – but I want to encourage you to dare to be different, I want to encourage you to belong to that group of people I often refer to as 'go-getters' or 'go-givers'. You see, people who don't stand for something will fall for anything, and I want to encourage you to make a stand; in fact, more than that, to actually step forward and stand out from the crowd.

Specifically, in this letter I want to talk to you about service, kindness and forgiveness: three attributes of a winner.

You see the real winners in life are always people of character. And character is something that comes from within, it is not something that can be taught with techniques. Character is like a wall or a building: it is built one brick at a time. For example, performing an honest act, in itself, does not create an honest character. It is only when people constantly act in ways that are honest that they can be considered to have developed an honest character. Character is developed over time. Each act of self-discipline, each stand for the truth, each decision to do what is right, each moral choice and each act of service may, in itself, be a small act, but over time these acts pile up one on top of another like bricks in a wall. Eventually the wall becomes a veritable rampart of strong character: a wall strong enough to withstand the many storms of life; a wall that offers support, shelter, strength, security and, also, success. You see, men and women of character tend to attract success. The following true story demonstrates the point well.

Many years ago in a small hotel in Philadelphia, USA, an elderly couple, on a business trip from England, approached the night clerk seeking a room. "We have tried several other hotels," said the man, "but it seems there is a convention in town and they are all full. Do you by any chance have a room you could let us have?"

The hotel clerk shook his head sadly and said, "I'm sorry, all our rooms are taken as well." Then, seeing the couple's dejected look, the clerk thought hard and came up with a suggestion: "Look, I will be working on the desk all night and so I don't need my room. Why don't you take that?" The couple were taken aback by his kindness and generosity, and after a little more persuasion they accepted his offer.

The next morning when they were checking out, the elderly man said to the clerk, "You would make a great hotel manager. How would you like it if I built a fine hotel in New York City and you came and managed it for me?" The clerk smiled politely and jokingly said, "Sir, I would like nothing better in the whole world."

They parted friends and the clerk thought nothing more about it until a couple of years later when he received a letter from the man, along with an invitation, an offer of a round-trip visit to New York to come and visit – guess what? – his new hotel. It turned out that the elderly gentleman was William Waldorf Astor, or Viscount Astor (the British peer). His hotel was the (now famous) Waldorf-Astoria on the corner of Fifth Avenue, in New York City. The clerk's name, the man who went the extra mile and dared to be different, was George C. Boldt. He became the Waldorf-Astoria's first manager and went on to become one of the greatest hotel managers in the world.

Being bothered, going the extra mile or daring to be different: that's what makes the winners in life stand out from the crowd; that's what determines success. The mark of all truly successful people, and businesses for that matter, is that they continually endeavour to serve others and make a positive difference, how ever great or small that difference may be. So, in fact, one of the greatest compliments anyone can bestow upon you is to acknowledge that you are different, set apart, special.

Many people talk about making a difference and many make promises, but making promises is like making babies; they are easy to make and often hard to deliver! Many people have the best intentions in the world but they fail to realise that it is action which makes the difference and not good intentions. Indeed, it has been said that you will be judged by your actions not your good intentions. It may be true that you have a heart of gold but there again, so does a hard-boiled egg.

It is action that counts, not lip-service. Read the following verse written by an anonymous author who certainly understood this truth.

I'd rather see a sermon than hear one any day;
I'd rather one should walk with me than merely tell the way.
The eye is a better pupil and more willing than the ear,
Fine counsel is confusing, but example is always clear.
For I might misunderstand you and the high advice you give,
But there's no misunderstanding how you act and how you live.
Anonymous

So, then, if you aspire to greatness, if you truly seek success and happiness, if you are determined to discover your true potential and live a life of fulfilment, dare to be different. Stand out from the crowd and go the extra mile in everything you do and say. Let people see your good intentions in action, not simply hear about them. Be a supporter of human kindness, be a positive influence on others around you, be a friend. Above all else, do your work with a dedication, pride and enthusiasm such as is rarely seen amongst most men or women and, in everything, provide platinum, knock-your-socks-off service that cannot help but be noticed. In a word, my friend, '*SHINE*'.

Now don't let these just be hollow words to you, don't let them inspire you as you read them and then expire as soon as you put these writings down. There are already far too many 'hollow' people out there. Hollow people kid themselves and others that they are something that really they are not. Many people are like that: on the outside they are big in material possessions and looks and so on, but on the inside they are empty, hollow and unfulfilled. That's because fulfilment in this world is never found in riches and material wealth alone; fulfilment is a by-product of self-sacrifice and service. You see, it is relatively easy to make a good living, but it's a lot harder to make a difference. So then, in your quest to discover your true potential and find lasting success, let me warn you against selfishness and empty pursuits. Instead, I want to encourage you to be a person of character, a person who stands out from the crowd and who dares to be different.

Among the many books in my library I have a special affection for the autobiography of Sam Walton, founder of the US company, Wal-Mart. Now, there was a man of character, a man who went the extra mile and who really did stand out from the crowd! Wal-Mart's company motto is this:

Who is the most important? The Customer.

Sam Walton lived by that motto. He believed in providing excellent value for money with knock-your-socks-off service, a philosophy which is held by his company to this day. For example, when entering a Wal-Mart store, customers are welcomed by what are called 'people greeters'. Employees are also trained to make eye contact with as many customers as possible and to offer assistance to anyone within ten feet, if they look as though they might need it.

Sam Walton began his company in 1945, when he borrowed $US20,000 from his father-in-law to open a small discount store in Arkansas. Today, Wal-Mart is the world's largest retailer with some 3,600 stores across the world. When he died in 1992, Sam

Walton had nearly a million employees and was one of the richest men in the world with a personal fortune in excess of $US20 billion. Yes, indeed, Sam Walton was a winner. He was a man of character, who believed in putting the customer first.

Cavett Robert is an author and speaker. He defines character this way:

> "Character is the ability to carry out a good resolution long after the mood in which it was made has left you."

Abraham Lincoln said:

> "Character is like a tree and reputation like its shadow. The shadow is what we think of it; the tree is the real thing."

In other words, your reputation is what others think about you but your character is who you really are. Some folk say that people can no more change their character than a leopard can change its spots but that, quite frankly, is not true. I believe that anyone can change their character if they really want to, as indeed I have changed mine. The key, of course, lies in wanting to change. If you want to change, I mean really WANT to change, then you will. On the other hand, if a person doesn't want to change then there is nothing in the world that will make him do so. Here is an example of the point in hand.

Last winter, during a heavy frost, I decided to start work later so that I could walk to school with two of my young children. I wanted to spend some time together with them, chatting, sliding on the ice, marvelling at the frosted beauty of the cobwebs and trees, and seeing icicles glistening in the early morning sun. On our walk we passed a bus shelter with what looked like a pile of rags laid out along the bench. The pile of rags turned out to be a tramp, a homeless vagrant, asleep in a drunken stupor in what appeared to be an attempt to shut out the world as well as the freezing cold. He was covered in the same deep frost that lay all around him, indicating that he had been there all night. My heart went out to him and so, after dropping my children off at school, I walked back the same way intent upon talking to this man and seeing if I could offer some help.

He is 49 years old and his name is Steven H. I still see him quite regularly. He is an alcoholic, homeless, jobless and in a state of poor health. Steven was once married but he divorced many years ago and no longer has any contact or relationship with any of his family or children. This is as much his own doing as it is theirs. He collects a little social security money each week and spends all of his days begging, scavenging for food and drunk on cheap liquor. This is the way that Steven chooses to live. He has done so for nine years and in that time has grown accustomed to it and, believe it or not, he is comfortable with it.

In other words, Steven doesn't want to change. Oh, if I asked him bluntly if he intends to die on the streets, he would say, "No," but when I ask him when he is going to accept help and change his situation he just shrugs his shoulders and smiles pathetically.

The thing is, I rather like Steven. Although with drink he sometimes gets a little out of hand, rebellious maybe, on the whole he is a likeable rogue who has unfortunately allowed himself to fall on hard times. On occasions I have talked to him, advised him and tried my utmost to get him to change. I have also fed him and clothed him and even taken him to the Social Services Department and talked with them about finding him a home. Nothing has worked and, unfortunately, it will not ever work until Steven decides that he wants to change. I cannot make that decision for him.

I still find it hard to accept that anyone could want to live like that, but he has resigned himself to the lifestyle, grown accustomed to it and the plain fact of the matter is, now, he doesn't really want to change. One thing that I have noticed about Steven, though, is that he responds to kindness. Most people just ignore him and walk on by, some are abusive towards him, others taunt him, but there are a few who show him kindness. As I have already mentioned, he is an alcoholic and sometimes he is rowdy or troublesome, but whenever I see him, his behaviour and attitude change.

Going back to my earlier point, then, a leopard may not be able to change its spots, but men and women can change themselves – if they really want to. The key lies in the wanting. The fact is, it is never too late to change. And if you want to change another person ... well, let me tell you, the easiest way to get results is by showing kindness in your thoughts, words and deeds. You see, people respond far more to kindness than to anything else. Think about it. If someone is kind to you or says a kind word to you, what is it that you want to do in return? Repay the compliment, right? Kindness seems to have a power of its own; it is almost magnetic. As Abraham Lincoln rightly said:

"A drop of honey catches far more flies than a gallon of gall."

Listen, now, to this beautiful piece of poetry written by Irishman, John Boyle O'Reilly (1844–1890):

What is Good?
"What is good?" I asked in musing mood.
Order, said the law court; Knowledge, said the school;
Truth, said the wise man; Pleasure, said the fool;
Love, said the maiden; Beauty, said the page;
Freedom, said the dreamer; Home, said the sage;
Fame, said the soldier; Equity, said the seer.
Then spoke my heart full sadly, "The answer is not here."
But then, from within my bosom, softly this I heard:
"Each heart holds the secret; Kindness is the word."
John Boyle O'Reilly

Let me illustrate the point further. Some time ago, a woman and her family moved to a small town. After she had been there for a few weeks the woman complained to her neighbour about the poor service she had received from the local shopkeeper and his surly attitude. (The newcomer was secretly hoping that her neighbour might speak to the owner on her behalf.)

Well, the very next time the woman had cause to visit the shop the owner greeted her with a warm smile and enthusiastically said how happy he was to see her again. He served her promptly and politely and remarked that he hoped she was settling in. The owner even offered his personal help and services to the woman and her family.

Amazed at the sudden transformation, she reported back to her friend all that had happened. "I suppose you told him how disappointed I was with his service?" she said. "Well actually, no," declared the neighbour. "I hope you don't mind but I told him you were very impressed with the way he had built up his small business and that his was one of the cleanest and best-run shops you had ever seen!"

The friendly neighbour understood, you see, that people respond far more to kindness than they do to anything else.

Aesop, the Greek slave and renowned writer of fables, who lived some 2,600 years ago, also knew this. His words have travelled across the centuries and are still as well-known today as they were back then. The sun can get you to take your coat off much quicker than the wind; and kindness, friendliness and appreciation will win people to your side far more readily than all the blustering and storming in the world. You might remember the story.

One day the sun and the wind got into a heated debate over which of the two was the more powerful. To settle the matter the wind suggested a test. "Do you see that old man walking along?" said the wind, "Let's see who can get his coat off the quickest!" So, out of nowhere, the wind suddenly attacked the man ferociously. It battered him and almost blew him off his feet as it ripped incessantly at his coat. But the old man just lowered his chin, pulled his coat tightly around him, and clutched on to it for all he was worth. Finally, exhausted by the effort, the wind gave up and it was the sun's turn.

Well, the sun shone kindly on the old man. The rays beamed down upon him and before long the old man mopped his forehead and then took off his coat. And the moral again, is this: people respond far more to kindness than to harshness.

Now, let me move on and say a word or two about forgiveness. You see, in this world of ours there are going to be people who hurt you, there is no doubt about that. However, you must learn to forgive people and not drop them or ignore them when they do something wrong or say something to upset you. You wouldn't discard your car or a bicycle if the tyre gets a puncture, would you? No. And how much more are people worth than machines? Remember, to err is human, to forgive divine.

If you remain unforgiving, if you harbour hurt and resentment in your heart, then these negative feelings will fester and eat away at you. They will hold you back. You see, resentment is carnivorous, it eats you alive; but forgiveness is a release. Some people forget to forgive – they hold on to resentment – but others forgive and forget. So don't ever allow resentment to get its teeth into you. When you feel its presence, shake it off, let go of it and move on. And remember this: if the forgiveness is not a mutual thing, let it be the other person's problem and not yours. Life is too short to allow others to hold you back.

Well, it's time once again to draw things to a close. In summary, then, I want to encourage you to be a person of character, I want to encourage you to dare to be different; to stand out from the crowd, to go the extra mile, to provide knock-your-socks-off service, to be kind, to be forgiving and above all else, to 'shine' like the bright light that you are meant to be.

And finally, a concluding thought to sign off with: Anne Frank, the holocaust victim, once wrote,

"How wonderful it is that nobody need wait a single moment before starting to improve the world."

Why not start afresh this very moment?

Until next time, I remain as always,

Yours cordially,
Uncle Bob

Chapter Thirteen
Getting Organised

The only one who got everything done by Friday was Robinson Crusoe.
Anonymous

Dear _ _ _ _ _ _ _ (fill in your name),

Imagine that every single morning when you awake someone gives you $1,440 in cash, so that you can build and save for the future. Let's say this same amount of money is automatically deposited into your private bank account, every single day, and it is yours to spend or invest as you please. However, there is just one string attached: any money that is not used will be taken back from you at the end of every day. In other words, any money you haven't invested or spent you don't get to keep. Now, if this were a real-life scenario, what would you do? You'd use every cent, wouldn't you? You would make sure that at the end of the day all the money had either been spent or invested wisely.

Well, guess what? You do, indeed, receive that exact same deposit each and every day. It is just that instead of receiving $1,440 in cash you receive 1,440 minutes (which is 24 hours). If you invest those minutes wisely you are building for the future, but any that are wasted or spent carelessly will be gone forever.

We often we hear the phrase 'time is money' and if you think of a day along those lines, as if it were an allotted sum of money that you either spend or invest, you will be sure to waste very little of it. You see, time is such a precious commodity. So much so that no one ever seems to have enough of it, and yet, so many people take it for granted and end up wasting much of the time they do have. For many others, of course, the complete opposite is true: they have so many things to do that they literally run out of time each day and so, as a consequence, they are constantly trying to make more and more time.

In this letter, then, I intend to look at this subject of time and give a perspective on how we can best use it. Hopefully, I will give you some direction and guidance as well as provoke you into thinking about how effectively you actually use your time. On that note, I have a little exercise for you to do.

I devised this simple self-appraisal exercise some time ago, and I occasionally use it in my workshops. My reasoning for incorporating it below is not to get you to pass judgement on yourself or to make you self-critical, but just to get you to think about how effectively you use your time. To that end, please answer the following questions honestly! Remember, this is not a test but a self-appraisal exercise. (That means, don't try to pick the option that you think will give you the best score!) After reading the questions consider each of the four options carefully and then, even if the choices do not entirely reflect how you feel, select whichever option is the most appropriate for you. Grab yourself a pencil before you start and put a tick by the letter corresponding to your answer. Here goes:

1. How often do you use a daily planner or 'things-to-do' list so that you can organise your workload effectively and prioritise your day?
    a) Frequently.
    b) Occasionally.
    c) Always.
    d) Hardly ever.

2. Regardless of what time you officially start work, when do you *actually* start work?
    a) I always start work straightaway.
    b) I have a cup of coffee first, but I start work soon afterwards.
    c) I tend to have a glance at the newspaper and maybe a chat to a few colleagues before I get going.
    d) I always seem to struggle to get started.

3. Is your working environment – your desk, office or place of work – orderly, is it neat and tidy?
   a) Yes. I am organised and I know where to find things.
   b) Mostly, but some days are better than others.
   c) No. I am always disorganised and can never find a thing.
   d) Not really. Most of the time it's an absolute shambles but I always manage to get through, somehow!

4. How do you handle interruptions or long-winded telephone callers?
   a) I tend to go along with the interruption for a while but will then hint that I am busy and hope the other party will get the message.
   b) I do not handle interruptions well and often allow others to control my time.
   c) I give it a few minutes and then make up an excuse to finish the conversation.
   d) I am always polite but assertive when dealing with interruptions.

5. After you have been interrupted how quickly do you get back to work?
   a) I never seem to be able to get going again once I have been distracted.
   b) Immediately.
   c) I tend to get sidetracked by the interruption and end up having to deal with whatever it is before I can get back to work again.
   d) I usually have a quick coffee break to gather my thoughts and then I am back into action.

6. Do you let people know when is the best time to contact you or how they can contact you?
   a) Most of the time
   b) Only now and then when I think about it
   c) Yes
   d) No.

7. How effectively do you handle paperwork?
   a) I keep picking it up, putting it down and picking it up again, until eventually it screams at me to deal with it.

b) I usually leave it till the last minute, but it always gets done.

c) I am always behind with my paperwork and I am often overwhelmed because I keep putting it off.

d) I try to deal with paperwork once, as soon as I get it.

8. How effectively do you delegate work or share out responsibility?

a) I delegate work when I need to.

b) I only delegate work if someone asks for more responsibility.

c) I delegate work whenever I can.

d) I never delegate my work: nobody else will do as good a job.

9. Are you punctual? Do you meet your deadlines? Do you arrive on time for meetings and appointments?

a) I am always on time, barring circumstances beyond my control.

b) I am usually on time.

c) I am late more times than not.

d) I am hardly ever on time.

10. Do you finish what you set out to do?

a) Always. I remain focused on the task at hand and stick with it until it is finished.

b) Eventually. I may have to keep coming back to it but I get there in the end.

c) Sometimes. I always set out with good intentions, but ...

d) Never. I never seem to be able to finish anything.

11. Do you allocate quality, uninterrupted time to family, leisure, exercise, rest and recuperation?

a) Occasionally, but not as often as I should.

b) No, I am just too busy and can't afford to do it at the moment, but things will change!

c) Yes, I prioritise time for these things.

d) I do set aside certain times for family, leisure, exercise, etc. but I am not always able to keep to it.

12. Can you relax and switch off?

a) No, I am a self-confessed workaholic and I can't switch off. I even take work home with me unnecessarily.

b) I can relax but then I feel guilty and start worrying that I should be doing something.
c) Most of the time I can relax and switch off but it takes me a while to unwind.
d) Yes, I can relax and switch off with relative ease.

13. Do you regularly set yourself personal goals?
a) I do set regular goals and every day I do something that in some way is getting me closer towards achieving them.
b) I have goals but I don't always work at them with the intensity that I should.
c) I set goals but I am not always disciplined enough to follow through with them.
d) I don't set goals because I tend to live each day as it comes.

14. How efficiently do you use your time?
a) I usually do the easy or 'fun stuff' first and leave the more important, 'not-so-fun stuff' until later.
b) I use my time efficiently to begin with but then I tend to slacken off as the day goes on.
c) I try to always make the most efficient use of my time.
d) I tend to always major in minors; I spend the majority of my time on minor tasks.

Now, using the following table, tot up your score and see just how effectively you do use your time.

1) a=3, b=2, c=4, d=1.	**2)** a=4, b=3, c=2, d=1.	
3) a=4, b=3, c=1, d=2.	**4)** a=2, b=1, c=3, d=4.	
5) a=1, b=4, c=2, d=3.	**6)** a=3, b=2, c=4, d=1.	
7) a=2, b=3, c=1, d=4.	**8)** a=3, b=2, c=4, d=1.	
9) a=4, b=3, c=2, d=1.	**10)** a=4, b=3, c=2, d=1.	
11) a=2, b=1, c=4, d=3.	**12)** a=1, b=2, c=3, d=4.	
13) a=4, b=3, c=2, d=1.	**14)** a=2, b=3, c=4, d=1.	

Total score

14–21: If you fall into this category then you are often completely overwhelmed and probably don't know whether you are coming or going. Most likely, you will be very frustrated and feel like giving up; you will lack energy, drive and determination and frequently wonder, *is it worth it?* More than anything else you lack purpose, direction and self-motivation. You need to ask yourself some serious questions, like, am I in the right field of work? (Go back and read Chapter 3, titled 'Purpose,' again.)

22–30: You are in dangerous territory and are starting to lose it. You are in a rut because you have accepted poor performance or, at best, mediocrity. If you don't get a grip and re-focus, if you don't pull yourself together and change your situation, then you will continue on a downward spiral until you eventually lose control all together. Don't allow that to happen. Read on.

31–39: 'Industry standard' is the best way to describe this group. In other words, you do a reasonable job and you manage to get by without causing too many waves. Around 80 per cent of people fall into this bracket, which can lull you into feeling this is acceptable. This, however, can be your biggest downfall. You see, you have the potential to go a lot further and achieve a great deal more. You can climb into the top 10 per cent if you will just push yourself and break out of the mould of 'standard performer'.

40–48: You have pretty much got it together. You manage your time effectively, for the most part, and you frequently achieve your objectives. Accomplishment is no stranger to you, but there again, you know that in some areas you are a lot better than in others. In this category the biggest danger to self-improvement is yourself. That is to say, you either are or can be your own worst enemy. You should understand that far too many people stop growing because they fall under the illusion of having already arrived! They are now enjoying success, they feel pretty good about themselves, they are happy; and consequently, they enter their comfort zone. This is where they stop learning and striving to improve and also, alas, where they inevitably begin to decline! Don't rest on your laurels. (According to the Collins English Dictionary, to rest on one's laurels is "to be satisfied with distinction won by past achievements and cease to strive for further achievements".) Don't do it, don't stop growing and striving to improve, because you, most definitely, have got what it takes to go all the way!

49–56: If you scored in this category then you either cheated in the test and scored yourself higher than you ought to have done, or else you really are in control. If this is your score then you make effective use of your time and you live by the saying: "Time flies; so it's up to me to be the navigator."

As I said earlier, the reason I have included this exercise is not to get you to pass judgement on yourself or to be self-critical but, rather, so that the questions might provoke you into thinking about just how effectively you do actually use your time. Regardless of your score, what is important now is the future, not the past! And the future – your future – every last minute of it, starts right now.

The fact is, we all have the exact same amount of time each day. The difference between those who succeed in life and those who don't is mainly determined by what they do with the amount of time they have. Now that doesn't mean we should simply work every hour that God sends. Indeed, as someone once said, "All work and no play makes Jack a dull boy ... and Jill a wealthy widow!"

Recently, I read a statement made by an anonymous but 'successful' businessman. This is what he wrote:

> "I have not seen the plays in town; only the computer printouts. I have not read the latest books, only the *Wall Street Journal*. I have not heard the birds sing this year, only the ringing of telephones. I have not taken a walk anywhere, except from the carpark to my office. I have not shared my feelings in years; but my thoughts are known to all. I have not listened to my own needs; but what I want I get. I have not shed a tear in years; but I have arrived. Is this really where I was going?"

What a price this man has paid for his so-called success. This reminds me of another man who said that he had spent his whole life climbing the ladder of success. When the day finally came and he reached the top, he looked around to survey the view and to his dismay, discovered that he had picked the wrong ladder! In other words, he had got his values all wrong.

In the book of Psalms in the Bible, Moses the Israelite leader, who lived some 3,500 years ago, wrote this prayer:

> "Teach us to number our days aright, that we may gain a heart of wisdom." (Psalm 90:12, NIV)

Another more modern translation says:

> "Teach me to number my days and recognise how few they are; and help me to spend them as I should." (TLB)

144

Let's now look at some more ways of doing just that.

At the beginning of this letter I said I would offer some direction and guidance as to how to use your time effectively. Of course, the exercise you have just completed hints at more than a few ways, but I now want to expand upon some of these. Let me give you some sound advice then, some sound advice by way of some sound-bites.

Organise, don't agonise

There is a well-known saying that goes like this: If you don't organise your day then someone else will. In other words, you must choose how you are going to spend your time, you must plan your day and stick to your plan diligently (barring any unforeseen and genuine emergencies, that is). If you don't discipline yourself to do this, then distractions will attack you from every angle in a relentless attempt to dictate how you will spend your time.

Allow yourself to soak up the words of this poem, written by Douglas Malloch, and determine that from this day forth, you will plan your time and time your plan:

There may be nothing wrong with you,
The way you live, the work you do,
But I can very plainly see
Exactly what is wrong with me.
It isn't that I am indolent
Or dodging duty by intent;
I work as hard as anyone,
And yet I get so little done,
The morning goes, the noon is here,
Before I know, the night is near,
And all around me, I regret,
Are things I haven't finished yet.
If I could just get organised!
I oftentimes have realised
Not all that matters is the man;
The man must also have a plan.
With you, there may be nothing wrong,
But here's my trouble right along;
I do the things that don't amount
To very much, of no account,

That really seem important though
And let a lot of matters go.
I nibble this, I nibble that,
But never finish what I'm at.
I work as hard as anyone,
And yet, I get so little done,
I'd do so much you'd be surprised,
If I could just get organised!

Douglas Malloch

There are many home truths in that verse, for all of us at times. If you identified with the poem, then make the decision right now to act. Just do it; do it right and do it right now.

Don't dawdle or procrastinate

Benjamin Franklin wrote:

"Dost thou love life? Then do not squander time, for that's the stuff life is made of."

So then, make the most of each moment. Yes, I know that is a lot easier to say than do, but imagine you only had an hour left to live; what would you do with it? Who would you phone? What would you say? Would you squander the hour wastefully or would you make the very best use of every minute? So then, make the most of the moment at hand. After all, no one knows just how many more they have left.

Former US ambassador (and child film star), Mrs Shirley Temple Black, relates a story about her husband Charles Black. When he was a boy, Charles apparently asked his mother what was the happiest moment of her life. His mother replied, "Why, this moment right now, dear, is the happiest moment of my life." The boy questioned her answer: "But what about things like getting married, buying your first home, having children? What about things like that?" Mrs Black answered, "My happiest moments of my life then were then, but my happiest moment now is now. You see, son, you can't live in the yesterdays or the tomorrows, you can only live each day as it comes."

A wise answer indeed. You should remember the yesterdays and plan for the tomorrows by all means, but live in the today and make sure you make the most of each moment.

Make a plan of action

As I have said before, things always feel much better when you have a plan to follow. Making a plan of action – whether that's creating a list of things to do or setting goals – gives you direction; it helps to focus your thoughts and energy, it provides you with an instruction manual and puts you in control of events rather than the other way round.

Without a plan of action you are laying yourself wide open to confusion, indecision, time-wasting and inefficiency. I remember an old rhyme from years ago about somebody who wanted to do so many things in life, but never got around to making any plans. Don't be like this guy:

> There was once an old sailor that my grandfather knew
> Who had so many things that he wanted to do
> But whenever he thought it was time to begin
> He couldn't because of the state he was in!

There is an often-quoted story about the multi-millionaire Charles Schwab (1862–1939) who was an associate of the famous industrialist and philanthropist Andrew Carnegie, and the one-time president of Bethlehem Steel Corporation in America.

During his time at Bethlehem Steel, Schwab brought in a highly respected management consultant, Ivy Lee, to see if he could come up with a plan to improve the company's performance and productivity. "We know what needs to be done," said Schwab, "We just need to know how we can do more of it. If you can show us a way to do that, then I will pay you handsomely."

"Well, that's not at all difficult," replied Lee. "Allow me to show you a simple procedure that will significantly increase your own personal effectiveness, and that of anyone else who chooses to use it."

The consultant then handed a blank piece of paper to Schwab and asked him to spend a moment or two listing down all the important tasks that he had to do the next day. When the list was finished, Lee then asked him to go back over the list and number each item in order of importance. Finally, Lee said, "Mr Schwab, first thing tomorrow you must start work on item number one on your list (the most important issue) and stick with it until you have finished. Then move on to item number two, then three and so on."

Lee went on to explain that some days it might not be possible to complete all the items on the list, but at least in following the method he would ensure that he was always tackling the most important issues. In any event, a great deal more would be accomplished with this daily procedure than without it. Lee further suggested that Mr Schwab try it out for himself first, and then if he discovered he was getting more things done, he should introduce the method to his workforce. Lee told Charles Schwab, "Try it for as long as you like and when you become convinced that this procedure works, send me a cheque for whatever value you think the idea is worth."

Some time later, Schwab sent Ivy Lee a thank you note along with a cheque for $25,000 (which is a great deal of money even today, but was worth far more back in the 1920s). Charles Schwab advocated that simple procedure as one of the best value for money lessons he had ever learnt. He used it every day and went on to create one of the largest steel companies in the world.

Now, if such success back then can be attributed to creating and following a daily plan of action, can't it do the same for you today? Of course, it can. All it takes is a little dedication and focus.

Focus

There is an old proverb that goes:

> A man with only one watch knows what time it is but a man with two is never quite sure.

In other words, you need to focus on the task at hand and not allow yourself to get sidetracked. Frankly, if you try to do too many things at once you become ineffective. So, then, focus on the task at hand and instead of watching the clock, copy its behaviour and keep on going until the job is finished.

Discipline

Harry Emerson Fosdick wrote:

> "No horse gets anywhere until it is harnessed. No steam or gas ever drives anything until it is confined. No Niagara is ever turned into light and power until it is tunnelled. And no life ever grows great until it is focused, dedicated and disciplined."

When he was in office as the US President, Harry S. Truman said,

"In reading the lives of great men, I found the first victory they won was over themselves. Self-discipline with all them came first."

Discipline or self-discipline: this is a very key matter in managing one's time effectively. Self-disciplined enough to stick to your agenda, self-disciplined to remain focused and not get distracted, self-disciplined to get into action when all you really want to do is mull around, and self-disciplined enough to say 'NO' when you really want to say 'yes'. Did you realise that the ability to say no to people or to things that put extra demands on your time is actually a mark of leadership? It takes a special strength of character to understand your capabilities and to say no, especially when what you really want to say all the time is yes. If this is a problem for you, if you keep getting sidetracked and giving in to other people's demands on your time, especially when you have more important things to do, then understand this: saying no is like riding a bike – you get better with practice.

Now, I am not suggesting that you start saying no to everyone or everything that requests or demands your time; that would hardly be compatible with the principles laid down in these writings. What I am suggesting is that you become self-disciplined enough to say no when you should say no.

Balance

This is another key issue in managing one's time effectively. If you want to avoid burn-out you must maintain a healthy balance between work, rest and play. This means dedicating time for work, but also time to spend on your spiritual life, time with your family and your friends, as well as time for exercise, recreation and rest. You must dedicate time for each regularly, even daily. Once again, this is very easy to say, I know, but as you have to admit, it is also very true. Ignore it to your own peril.

In the final analysis, there will be times when there is just not enough time in the day to get everything done. That much is fact. However, if you don't maintain a healthy balance the day will come, sooner than it should, when you literally won't have any time left at all! So do yourself a favour, get your priorities right and do it now, not tomorrow.

Priority

Ask yourself this: a week from now, a month from now or a year from now, will it really matter if _ _ _ _ _ _ _ _ (you fill in the space) doesn't get done? The fact is, we each determine how we will spend our time – for the most part, at least – and I want to encourage you to prioritise and spend yours wisely on the stuff that is *really* important.

William Gladstone (1809–98), the British statesman, spent 60 years in British politics and served as Prime Minister on four separate occasions. As such, he was a man who had enormous demands on his time and who had to learn how to prioritise. Gladstone once said:

> "He is wise who wastes no time on pursuits for which he is not fitted, and he is wiser still who from among the things he can do well, chooses and then resolutely follows the best."

Throughout these writings I have advocated that you always finish what you have started, that you stick with a job and see it through to the end, no matter what. I am not about to contradict that. However, there are times when we can all get a little stubborn and pedantic about finishing a particular job, a minor issue, when there are far more important things beckoning us. What am I saying? Simply this: you need to prioritise your time.

For example, did you really have to stay late at the office last night to finish that report, I mean *really*? Couldn't you have prioritised your time better? Couldn't you have decided it was more important to go home and read the children a bedtime story than it was to leave the office with a tidy desk? You could always have gone into work a half-hour earlier this morning to finish it off. Remember this: no one on their deathbed ever said, "I wish I had spent more time at the office."

We all prioritise our time. It is high time that we should get our priorities right. And on that note, it is now time for me to sign off and join my wife for lunch. Until next time then, I remain as always,

Yours cordially
Uncle Bob

Chapter Fourteen

Family Affairs

If you want your children to turn out well, spend twice as much time with them, and half as much money on them.
(Attributed to Abigail Van Buren, advice columnist 'Dear Abby')

Dear _ _ _ _ _ _ (fill in your name),

Following on from my last letter, I want to say a few more words about investing time with your family; particularly your spouse and/or your children (if you have them). I say 'investing' rather than 'spending' because having time for your family is exactly that, an investment in your relational future. Now, as we have already touched upon this subject several times before, I shall not be writing at any great length here. However, I would ask you to appreciate that it is not the length of this letter that is important, as much as the content. There is little point in writing many words when just a few will have a greater effect. After saying that, it is only now, after we have spent a considerable amount of time together, that I am able to write a shorter letter and not compromise on the quality of our time.

There is a good analogy here. When it comes to spending time with family, many 'busy' people say that it's the quality of the time that counts and not so much the quantity of time. But that is not entirely accurate. You see, we can only enjoy quality time with people after we have invested a considerable *quantity* of time with them. The quality time comes only after the investment of quantity. The first point I want to make then is this: if you want to enjoy quality time with your family, if you want to have a happy home, a spouse with whom you can share a loving relationship, and children who will love you, respect you and who will 'turn out well,' then you have to spend time with them; a lot of time with them.

Yes, I know this is often difficult, and I know there are pressures and commitments all screaming at you and vying for your precious time. Indeed, there will be occasions when work commitments will make it nigh on impossible to find any time at all for your loved ones. Of course, we all have to work and sometimes our work must take priority, otherwise we wouldn't be able to support our family. But understand this: there is a major difference between the words 'sometimes' and 'all the time'. Many men, especially, do not heed this advice. Some men are always at work. They love it because their work gives them a sense of achievement and fulfilment; it stimulates them, rewards them and provides recognition. In itself, work like this is a wonderful blessing, but not at any price. This quote, from an anonymous source, about sums it up:

> "Our families should be our top priority. No other success can compensate for failure at home."

Author, Dr James Dobson, in his book *Straight Talk to Men*, quotes some recent research done in America to determine how much time middle-class fathers spent interacting with their small children. It does not make for happy reading! The researchers asked a group of fathers how much time they estimated they spent each day with their children. The average answer was between 15 and 20 minutes a day. To establish how accurate these claims were, the researchers then attached a small recording device to the children's clothes so that they could monitor exactly how much interaction went on. On average, the time spent by these middle-class fathers interacting on a one-to-one basis with their young children amounted to just 37 seconds a day! And the average time spent in direct interaction in any given encounter amounted to just 10 to 15 seconds at a time. Dr Dobson also quotes various other studies that cite pre-school children spending between 30 and 50 hours a week in front of the television screen (or computer).

I know that I, for one, do not want my children to become a part of those statistics. You see, I grew up without a father and so when I became one myself I was, and still am, determined to be a *real* father to my children and to spend as much time as I can with them. I remember a few years ago, however, when things started to slip. I was busy at work with more than my fair share of problems and I felt bad that I was not spending as much time with my children as I would have liked. I remember it was January, and as a New Year's resolution I decided that I would spend at least an hour a day, every day, with my children. Now, I am the stubborn, strong-willed type and so when I set the target of an hour a day, I was determined to stick with it, come what may. And stick with it I did, although, I am ashamed to say, it was often with reluctance and with me clock-watching and calculating how many of the 60 minutes were left because I had other things I needed to do. As well, for a little while I fell into the trap of thinking that being in my children's company, or in the same room as them, was the same as spending time with them.

Then one night – I remember it as though it were yesterday – I sat in the bathroom, clock-watching, while the children played happily in the bath together. I was in a silent, sullen mood and I was giving my hour reluctantly; fighting my conscience by telling myself that I had spent most of the previous day with them and I could always make up for it tomorrow or the day after that. After a little while my then five-year-old daughter, Kimberley, looked up at me with her big blue eyes full of sadness, and her words pierced my heart as she said in a mimicking voice, "Daddy, if you can't spend quality time with us it would be better if you didn't spend any time at all."

I learnt two very important lessons that day:

1. That children, even as young as five, really do pick up the values of their parents. Wherever had a five-year-old picked up the concept of quality time, if not from myself?

2. Being in the same place as my children is not the same as actually spending time with them.

Read the following poem written by an unknown dad; it's a poem about his son and about how important it is for him to set an example his son will follow. Read it and decide to invest your time wisely – now – with your own children. Remember this: the more time you spend with your children when they are young the more time they will want to spend with you when you are old.

A careful man I want to be,
For a little fellow follows me.
I do not dare to go astray,
For fear he'll go the self-same way.

I cannot once escape his eyes.
Whatever he sees me do – he tries.
Like ME – he says he's going to be,
That little chap who follows me.

I must remember as I go,
Through summer sun and winter snow,
That I am building for the years to be;
That little chap who follows me.

Anonymous

Of course, just as important, if not more so, is investing time in your marriage. After all, your spouse is the person you have planned to spend the rest of your life with. Too many marriages go stale simply because of a lack of investment in each other; in spending time together doing the things that you both want to do. This, again, is probably particularly pertinent to men. Busy men would do well to heed the warning in this old saying: "The man who is always as busy as a bee might one day wake up to discover that someone has stolen his honey!" Make time for your wife or husband; real time – quality time.

Marriage is defined as a unity, a joining together of two people, a man and a woman, to become as 'one flesh'. A husband must not, therefore, dominate his wife nor should a wife dominate her husband. If they are of 'one flesh' and love each other, as they should, then they have a common purpose; to be there for each other and to serve the other's needs.

In the story of Adam and Eve in the Bible, God says, "It is not good for man to be alone. I will make a helper suitable for him." (Genesis 2:18) God did not say "I will make a servant or a slave for him," he did not say "I will make a worker for him," but God said a helper, someone to share with. In the *New Bible Commentary* (21st Century Edition, published by IVP) it says this:

> "'Suitable helper' would be better translated 'helper matching him,' i.e. supplying what he lacks. She is his missing rib.

> Matthew Henry (1662–1714) commented on God's choice of a rib to create Eve, 'Not made out of his head to top him, not out of his feet to be trampled upon by him, but out of his side to be equal with him, under his arm to be protected, and near his heart to be beloved.'"

Now, I need to nail my colours to the masts, here, and state that I believe in the biblical teaching that a man is meant to be the head of the family (Ephesians 5: 22–28). That is not to say that a man's role is somehow more important, but I do believe that he should take the lead. And leadership, true leadership, means one thing – servitude.

At the end of the day, you can only get out of a marriage what you put into it. It's like a bank account: sometimes you are allowed to overdraw but unless you pay back with interest you will eventually go bankrupt. Now call me a sentimentalist, but I love this description of what it means to be married. It is a piece of prose written by T.D. Jakes:

> "To the one you marry you are saying, 'When my time comes to leave this world, when the chill of eternity blows away my birthdays and my future stands still in the night, it's your face I want to kiss good-bye. It's your hand I want to squeeze, as I slip from time to eternity. As the curtain closes on all I have attempted to do and be, I want to look into your eyes and see that I mattered. Not what I looked like or how much money I made, or even how talented I was. I just want to look into the eyes of someone who loved me and see that I *mattered*.'"

Let me say it again: make time for your spouse, real time, quality time. Gaining success and wealth in business is wonderful and fine, but not if you don't have anyone to share it with. In other words, your purpose in this life, no matter how important, does not entail neglecting your family. It is one thing striving to achieve success and riches; it's another striving to achieve a happy home and a loving family. The key to winning in both areas is a thing called 'balance'. Billy Graham said it well with this statement:

> "There is nothing wrong with men possessing riches. The wrong comes when riches possess men."

You know, in the Bible there are around 2,300 references to money and possessions (obviously someone thought the subject was important!) but there are many more references to family. Likewise, then, we should get our priorities right!

I said that this would be a short letter because there seems little point in writing many words when a few will have a greater effect. I believe that I have now said enough to make you think and to encourage you to take action.

Let me finish off, then, by sharing a final analogy with you. This is a piece of writing (attributed to T. J. Watson) that talks about 'team effort'. Now team effort – that is, having balance or sharing the load – is exactly what it takes to run a successful business and also, a successful marriage. I have adapted the prose slightly to emphasise this point.

> "When you see geese flying along in 'V' formation, you might consider what science has discovered as to why they fly that way. As each bird flaps its wings, it creates an up-lift for the bird immediately following. By flying in 'V' formation, the whole flock has a 71 per cent greater flying range than if each bird flew on its own."

(A husband and wife who share a common direction and sense of family togetherness can get where they are going more quickly and easily because they are travelling on the thrust of one another.)

> "When a goose falls out of formation, it suddenly feels the drag and resistance of trying to go it alone – and quickly gets back into formation to take advantage of the lifting power of the bird in front."

(If we have as much sense as a goose, we will stay in formation with our spouse and those people who are headed in the same direction we are; we will also be willing to accept their help and give of ourselves to others.)

> "When the head goose gets tired, it goes to the back of the 'V' and another goose flies point."

(It is sensible to take turns doing demanding jobs, whether you're a person or a goose flying south.)

> "Geese honk from behind to encourage those up front to keep up their speed."

(We need to make sure that when we honk from behind it is to offer encouragement and not something else!)

> "Finally – and this is important – when a goose gets sick or wounded, or shot down, other geese fall out of formation and follow it down to offer support and protection. They stay with the fallen goose until it is able to fly or until it dies, and only then do they launch out on their own, or with another formation to catch up with their group."

(If we have the sense of a goose, we will stand by each other like that.)

In closing, let me say it once more: invest time with your family, real time, quality time.

Well, you now have all the ammunition you need to '*Discover Your True Potential*' and realise your heart's desires. I wish you well, and, in signing off this final time, let me leave you with an old Irish blessing:

> May there always be work for your hands to do,
> May your purse always hold a coin or two.
> May the sun always shine warm on your windowpane,
> May a rainbow be certain to follow each rain.
> May the hand of a friend always be near you,
> And may God fill your heart with gladness to cheer you.

May God bless you in your endeavours and until next time, my friend, good luck to you and goodbye for now.

Yours cordially,
Uncle Bob

Postscript

Dear _ _ _ _ _ _ _ (fill in your name),

If you have read my book *One on One: The Secrets of Professional Sales Closing*, you will know that I have a philosophy in life; namely, if you don't ask you don't get. I would like to ask something of you.

Having now read *Discover Your True Potential*, it is my sincere hope that you have found it to be both encouraging and, more importantly, helpful. This was, after all, my intention in writing it. If you have found this to be so, and in some way the words contained in this book have inspired you, then I would like to ask that you do something for me. Would you please pass the message on and recommend this book to others?

I know from experience that the best form of advertising is word-of-mouth recommendation. It is my desire that this book be as widely read as possible, not so that I will earn more money from it (if you have read this book you will know that statement to be true), but so that *Discover Your True Potential* can do for others what I hope it has done, and will continue to do, for you. I would like to add that if you know of an individual who cannot afford to buy this book but who needs to read it, or if at the present time you cannot afford to buy a copy for them yourself, then please let them borrow this one.

Yours sincerely,
R. Ian Seymour (alias Uncle Bob)

Index

Contact Details

Ian Seymour is available internationally for speaking engagements, in-house sales, management and personal development training, seminars and consultancy appointments. He is also very happy to hear from his readers.

Would you like Ian to be part of your next meeting, conference, think-tank or training class? You can contact him by visiting his website, www.seymour-results.com, by email to ian@seymour-results.com, or by writing to:

Ian Seymour
SEYMOUR RESULTS
P.O. Box 3019 Wokingham
Berkshire RG40 4GA
England